Dedicated to Mahmood Kavir

Without whose help and guidance
this translation would not have been possible

Copyright © 2013 Bahiyeh Afnan Shahid.

All rights reserved. No part of this book may be used or reproduced by any means, graphic, electronic, or mechanical, including photocopying, recording, taping or by any information storage retrieval system without the written permission of the publisher except in the case of brief quotations embodied in critical articles and reviews.

Balboa Press books may be ordered through booksellers or by contacting:
Balboa Press
A Division of Hay House
1663 Liberty Drive
Bloomington, IN 47403
www.balboapress.com
1-(877) 407-4847

Original 1st edition: Beyond Art Production, London
Copy editor: Katia Hadidian, London
Original design: Normal Industries, Germany

Because of the dynamic nature of the Internet, any web addresses or links contained in this book may have changed since publication and may no longer be valid. The views expressed in this work are solely those of the author and do not necessarily reflect the views of the publisher, and the publisher hereby disclaims any responsibility for them.

Printed in the United States of America.

ISBN: 978-1-4525-7147-8 (sc)
ISBN: 978-1-4525-7149-2 (hc)
ISBN: 978-1-4525-7148-5 (e)
Library of Congress Control Number: 2013906112

Balboa Press rev. date: 4/10/2013

Sohrab Sepehri

A selection of poems from
The Eight Books

Translated by Bahiyeh Afnan Shahid

Contents

About the Translation 6

Doors Of Awareness 8
by Bahiyeh Afnan Shahid

Sepehri: An Appreciation 16
by Mahmood Kavir

Glossary 162

From Book I: The Death of Colour 23
In the Pitch Black of Night
Smoke is Rising
Dawn
The Riddle Bird
A Light at the Heart of Night
Mirage
Towards Sunset
Sorrowful Sadness
Ruin
One Who Revives
The Silent Valley
Dang
A Man and the Sea
The Death of Colour
A Happening
An Image

From Book II: The Life of Dreams 41
The Wet Lantern
The Lotus Flower
Journey

From Book III: Burden of the Sun 49
Without Warp and Weft
You Who Are So Close
The Mirror Flower
The Dust of a Smile
Another Realm
We Are the Shady Bower of Our Tranquillity
Travelling Companion

From Book IV: East of Grief 63
Haay
Doubt
No to Stone
And
Na
My Fervour
Bodhi
Something Happened
Until
Till the Flower of Naught

From Book V: Sound of the Footsteps of Water 77
Sound of the Footsteps of Water

From Book VI: The Traveller 95
The Traveller

From Book VII: Green Mass 111
Over Eyelids of the Night
Light, Flowers, Water and I
A Message to Come
Plain Coloured Water
Golestaneh
Lonely Exile
The Fish Were Saying
Where is the House of the Friend?
An Oasis Within an Instant
Beyond the Seas

Heartbeat of a Friend's Shadow
Songs of a Visit
A Good Night of Loneliness
Feathers of a Song
The Sura of Contemplation
A Sun
Stirrings of the Word 'Life'
The Illuminated Page of Time
From Green to Green
Forever
The Initial Call
To the Garden of My Fellow Travellers
Friend
Till the Wet Pulse of Morning

From Book VIII: We are Nothing but a Gaze 147
Oh Fervour, Oh Ancient One
The Tender Time of Sand
Beyond the Waters
Both Line and Space
Ancient Text of Night
No Dolls in Our Days
Eyes of a Rite of Passage
Solitude of a Scene
Towards the Beloved's Imaginings
Here Always 'Teeh'
Till the End in Audience

5

About the Translation

As an Iranian who has spent the greater part of my life outside Iran, I came to the study of Persian poetry late in life. It was a desire to read poets such as Rumi and Hafez in the original Farsi, with which I was not yet very conversant, that sent me in search of a teacher. By sheer chance my path crossed that of Dr Mahmood Kavir – an academic, writer, historian and poet who had taught at Tehran University and who, like many like him, was an exile in Britain. The 'teaching' turned out to be multifaceted. First, there was the hurdle of fluency in the language – Dr Kavir's method was a gentle but total plunge into the intoxicating world of the *ghazals* (an ancient poetic form similar to sonnets) of Hafez. This was followed by those of Mowlana Jalal-u-Deen Rumi (or Balkhi, since he was born in Balkh), set against a panorama of Persian literature and related history, ranging from Roudaki in the 10th century to modern times.

For me, an Iranian born in Palestine, educated there, in Lebanon and the US, and who during the course of my lifetime had lived in Haifa, Beirut, Washington DC, Paris and London, this was a very special homecoming. I was, in more ways than one, very literally an exile: an Iranian who had never done more than visit Iran, who did not yet have a very good command of the language, but who yet had the nostalgia of the exile for the cultural, if not geographic, homeland of generations past. Above all, it was a spiritual homecoming, deftly and naturally brought about by a teacher deeply immersed in the ultimate pilgrimage of the Sufi on the road of what in Farsi is called *irfan* – gnosis, or the way back to the Beloved – so integral to the wholeness of a human being and from which humankind tends to be alienated. Reading and rereading the *ghazals*, listening to them set to music or just read out loud, it soon became apparent that the flowing, magical rhymes, cadences, lines and lyrics of the poetry were primarily a lovely means of conveying a highly charged, emotionally intense longing of the human heart, searching for a way out of the tunnel of the material and the mundane to the inner land of liberation and illumination.

For centuries, this searching – and in some cases, the finding – had been going on, sometimes openly, sometimes secretly; at times well received, at others heavily attacked – and understandably so, for it insisted upon freeing the human spirit, soul and mind from the shackles of both Sheikh and Shah (Church and State), an idea that often produced 'undesirable' truths.

By the time Sohrab Sepehri took up the thread in the last century, he too was criticised, which probably contributed to the somewhat convoluted way he presented some of his poetry. However, in spite of that, this modern-day *aref* (mystic), poet and painter is convincingly sincere in his heart-felt and touching approach to the way we must look at our world, and our fellow humans, in these stressful, problematic times.

For me, *irfan* was an infectious challenge; one that opened new vistas, new visions and journeys. The rich cavalcade of poets who had used their art to express this deep-seated, high-flying longing of the human heart had one of its 20th-century expressions in the work of Sohrab Sepehri. A translation that aspires to do him justice, no matter how far short it falls, seems to be the least of tributes that could be offered in his name.

Bahiyeh Afnan Shahid

Doors of Awareness

The Iranian poet and painter Sohrab Sepehri was born in Kashan, Iran, in 1928, and was claimed by cancer in 1980. He had an upbringing that tried to discipline and shape him, whether at home or at school, but he was not exactly a conformist. He was an intelligent, sensitive, artistically gifted, poetically expressive, somewhat withdrawn, soft-spoken human being. Never married, widely travelled whenever finances permitted, he visited Japan – where he studied woodcut techniques – China, India, Pakistan, Afghanistan, Greece, Egypt, Austria, Italy, France, Britain (for medical treatment) and the United States. Some he visited more than once, and for a time he lived in the United States and France. He tried his hand at stage design, as well as translating old Chinese and Japanese poetry into Farsi.

Sepehri started painting and writing poetry at an early age. At both he excelled. For both he received acclaim and criticism. Now he is enshrined as one of the foremost Iranian poets and painters of the 20th century.

During his lifetime, a great many changes came about, not only in Iran and the Middle East, but all around the world. Many of the norms of life – that is, the 'traditional' way of doing things – changed, sometimes drastically, sometimes gradually. Whether it was child rearing, education, marriage, work, society, politics or religion, they went through metamorphoses and change, often of a rather drastic, 'shocking', or maybe even 'blasphemous' kind. Thousands of questions were raised, and thousands of answers were suggested, simply because there was an urgent need for them.

One such was provided by Sohrab Sepehri. Doubtless the outcome of his own penetrating and ever-questioning search, he found that the answers were all around him. His two main sources of insight were nature – which is why he is sometimes described as a 'nature mystic' – and a very long mystical tradition, which was not only larger than life, but where one, 'on the waters of providential guidance... rowed until the full manifestation of wonder and awe', and where, 'One must sit, close to the unfolding, some place between rapture and illumination.'

Seemingly unaffected and uninvolved in what was happening around him, he turned inward, and in his own mind and heart worked out the answers that to him appeared suitable and satisfactory for many of the problems that prevailed.

His solution lay in a new look at humanity in its natural habitat, at one with nature, acting and reacting with a creation that was alive with water, light, soil and sun, plant and animal life. These had personalities and characters of their own, with which people could feel, interact and relate, as parts of a totality full of beauty and vitality. Having changed the way one looked at everything around made it easier for categories and divisions to fall away, and the underlying unity of being to become visible and palpable.

To be able to 'see' that way, Sepehri started with an old mystic tradition, a favourite symbol: the cleansing of the mirror of the heart. That was where the journey started and ended. The necessary preamble was to 'break free of the caravan' of the norm and the accepted, and to launch on a road that took the 'restless wayfarer from the road of illusions' – illusions about material needs, greed, power – and allowed him to step into 'an enchanted land' where he turned away from the road of delusion.

Sepehri does not make for easy reading, particularly as the imagery that he uses is so very special to him. However, when one has established a bond with him, his words and images come alive, his plea to the *houris* to 'wash away from my sight the blinding spell' rings true and ceases to be a poet's imagination. One finds that, indeed, 'a silver key has been turned', that 'the door of awareness has opened', and that one has truly 'stepped into an enchanted land'. Here one can join him when he says 'at the edge of dew let us stand, alight on a leaf'. You can believe him when he says, 'a poppy plant has bathed me in the flow of being'. The simple reality for Sohrab Sepehri is that this enchanted land is no fairytale, but the landscape of everyday life and living, close to nature, where 'snow sits on the shoulder of silence' and 'Time on the spine of a jasmine flower'. He does not speak of poetic fancies but what for him are true realities, where even laughter can 'cast stark shadows' and where his 'restless hands ... stretched toward a fruit, do not denote a desire to despoil, but a thirst for friendship'. He speaks of 'sadness in search of a smile', of his 'heart saddened in sunset tightness', where:

> Continuity that pours poison in my veins
> Depriving me of the idea of the here and now
> And from far and distant places
> Binds me to thoughts of decay and decline.
> From 'Dang'

Sepehri repeatedly spoke of his loneliness, of 'inner desolation', of the 'search for awareness'. He could be misjudged as a poet wallowing in self-pity, but the protagonist in his real-life drama was humanity, rather than he himself. His experience, his new way of seeing things, brings him to the point where the sanctity and the simplicity of life, of awareness of the world of nature, of human relationships, of the 'closeness of God among these scented stocks, at the foot of that tall pine tree', where 'living was like a repeated shower of happiness, a plane tree full of starlings', became the central point of existence.

For him, being, existence, awareness, and ever-progressive maturity were of the essence. He stated it very simply in one phrase: 'As long as poppies bloom, life must be lived.' The aptness of his approach to materialism, commercialism, environmental despoiling, money and power, takes one back to the sacredness of nature, the oneness of all the diversity within it, and humanity as an integral, interconnected, interdependent part of it.

Surveying both the mysticism and mythology of the East, whether Japanese, Chinese or Indian, Iranian or Islamic, he seemed to conclude – as many others had done before him – that humanity had lost touch with the original innocence that prevailed in Paradise, and its task in this world was to regain that condition. The way to do this was through a new understanding of nature, our place in it and as an integral part of creation, to develop a clear awareness of the oneness of being. As human beings, one major step was to realise the divine potential within us – a potential that exists in everyone, and maybe in everything – if only allowed to come to fruition. Some of the hurdles are the many masks that upbringing, schooling, peer pressure, society, religion and politics impose on people. All this layering disguises the original spirit and soul that we are born with – our original heritage, our birthright dowry. Sepehri's suggestion? Surrounded and in touch with nature, take a deep breath and wash your eyes and soul from the overlaying masks. Look within and see what reality and beauty reside there. Look without, and see how akin it is.

Considering the 'inner desolation' that we can sometimes suffer, Sepehri suggests that we should 'break free from the caravan'. But for this breaking away, there is a price to pay, for here the 'resounding of the cup of loneliness' is heard, though not without the knowledge that 'beauty and suffering are its warp and weft'. Here is 'sadness in search of a smile', but also 'a tune that bursts open the grave of my mind'. He even envisions a blossoming in the valley of death – death of self – which for him was not a place of 'darkness and loneliness' but 'a beautiful retreat' where regeneration occurs.

In a brief comparison with Jalal-u-Deen Rumi, the great master and mystic sage of the 13th century, we find that while Rumi calls upon one to soar high in the skies of passionate dedication, en route to the lost Paradise and encounter with the Beloved, Sepehri, mild-mannered and quiet, casts an even-tempered and balanced look on a clarified humanity in harmony with nature. While Rumi sings of flight and freedom, Sepehri hums of the lightening of the worldly burden, and of gently floating into a world of awareness and fine-tuned understanding. The mystic of the 20th century seeks a light that radiates from the individual soul, and ultimately affects its relationship with others and the world around it. The mystic in Rumi dances, sings and chants out loud that he comes from the world of spirit, and is a stranger in the world of matter. Sepehri, quietly aware of humanity in a milieu alien to its physical, psychological and spiritual needs, in poetry and in painting, appeared to stroke human consciousness into a tranquility, almost a state of beatitude, which nevertheless is never quite free of the ongoing struggle for 'understanding, awareness, illumination'.

One can almost picture him, wavy black hair atop a gaunt face; dark, pained eyes; a black beard and moustache; thin body, from hollow cheeks to hollow chest and hollow belly, drawing his unusually long fingers over the psyche of humanity, simply, gently, lovingly. In his own quest, he set out from the 'freshness of the emerald garden of childhood', from which the sand castles of those days 'had been washed away by the rain'. The youth, though, deviated from the path of maturity and illumination and, like Sepehri, realised and hastened to proclaim that 'My place is not here!' since:

> The whisperings of the night grow in my veins
> The drunken, moss-coloured rain
> Drips on the thirsty walls of my soul.
> I am a star that has fallen in drops
> From 'The Wet Lantern' (*Fanouseh Kheece*)

So he calls out:

> *Rise up, rise up. Break the line of vision,*
> *break the black delusion.*
> *I have come, I have come. Another wind is blowing,*
> *another scent is in the air.*
> *This is not your town, this is not your town.*
> *Your town is in higher regions, in other valleys'.*
> From 'Until' (*Ta*)

In such a place, 'to the eternity of flowers we are linked'. He advises that 'the brightness of your eyes to the safe-keeping of sand and stars bestow' (from 'Another Realm', *Diyari Deegar*).

If you do so, then:

> *You have stepped into an enchanted land*
> *Your eyes overflowing with misty images!*
> *Open your tightly closed doors*
> *For hidden veils to come alive in the dance*
> *of an intoxicating perfume*
> From 'The Mirror Flower' (*Golleh Ayeneh*)

Seeing himself on an almost prophetic mission, Sepehri claimed that:

> *One day*
> *I shall come and a message I shall bring...*
> *Clouds I shall tear apart*
> *Eyes with the sun I shall entwine, hearts with ishq,*
> *shadows with water, branches with the wind*
> From 'A Message to Come' (*Peyami Dar Rah*)

Nor was all this to be achieved through deep religiosity, extreme asceticism or turning away from the world and what it contains. To him, it appeared that the child had been thrown out and the bath water retained. It was the 'dust' of everyday experience that he wanted washed away from eyes, to be free to go in search of that lotus flower from which Being was born, and which Sepehri sees as having roots in him. That lotus flower,

> ... had permeated my life
> It was I who was running through its veins
> Its existence had roots in me.
> From 'Journey' (*Safar*)

The object of the whole exercise was to arrive at a point where:

> The doors of awareness have opened.
> At the entrance a moment of dread fell away.
> At the edge of the spellbound night,
> the shadows of hesitation fell apart
> The doorway of vision drank of the haze of light.
> From 'The Mirror Flower' (*Golleh Ayeneh*)

Attempting to translate Sohrab Sepehri has turned out to be a pilgrimage. You start something that you feel needs to be done, but in so doing you give yourself over to the 'wayfarer's path' and before you know it, you are aiming for the goals that he describes and so strongly believes in. You are affected, changed, maybe even shaped by the process. At the end, you realise that it has not been a labour of choice, but a response 'to a voice that called'.

Bahiyeh Afnan Shahid

Sepehri: An Appreciation

By contemplation I swear,
By the beginning of speech,
By the flight of a dove from the mind.
A word is in the cage

From 'We Are Nothing But a Gaze' (*Ma Heech, Ma Negah*)

The artist, poet and mystic Sohrab Sepehri wrote eight slim volumes of poetry in his lifetime: *Death of Colour* (1951); *The Life of Dreams* (1953); *Burden of the Sun* (1961); *East of Grief* (1961); *Sound of the Footsteps of Water* (1965); *The Traveller* (1966); *Green Mass* (1967); and *We Are Nothing But a Gaze* (1977). The selection of poems in this volume is from a collection of these works, the *Eight Books of Sohrab Sepehri* (1977).

When Sepehri started writing, Iran was going through one of the more troubled periods in its history. On the one hand, political and intellectual aspirations and agitations tried, but were unable to achieve, their goals, while on the other, royal 'reforms' disrupted many of the social institutions of the country. That did not seem to affect Sepehri, however, a poet with a deep and abiding faith in a brighter future and a more promising tomorrow.

Though universal in his appeal, Sepehri's heart was in Kashan, and though from Kashan – a city in the province of Isfahan – he did not consider himself just a Kashani. He was a citizen of the world: the earth was his home, humanity his people, his religion, *ishq* (man's passionate mystical love for the Beloved).

I am from Kashan, but
Kashan is not my hometown.
My hometown is lost.
I, with patience, with fervour
Built another on the other side of Night.

From 'Sound of the Footsteps of Water' (*Sedayeh Payeh Ab*)

Kashan is the green emerald of the Kavir desert. Kashan is the blue of luscious, bubbling springwater that flows from the heart of Kavir's thirst. Kashan is not a city. It is a large rural area with a small town of mud-walled houses and roofs, a profusion of pomegranate trees, orchard paths full of red roses, the home of memories, perfume and pears, the land of silk and hand-woven carpets. The magic of Kashan, larger than life and as wide as the world, is clearly visible in the concepts and ideas that mark Sepehri's poetry. High roofs burning in the sun, shady courtyards full of Seville orange and pomegranate trees, pools of water, fountains of entreaty, water lilies that beckon you both into yourself and outward to humanity's birthday party, the fall of mankind from Paradise to God's sacred garden, to the blue springs of the sky, to praise and benediction, to humanity's resplendent song. A humanity that, in his eyes, recognises no frontiers, is enchanting and worships at the temple of nature.

> *My Mecca is a red rose,*
> *My prayer rug a spring of water, light my seal.*
> *The plain my place of prayer.*
> *I perform my ablutions with the throbbing of the windows.*
> *In my prayer flows the moon, flows a river of colour.*
> *Stones can be seen through my prayers.*
> From 'Sound of the Footsteps of Water' (*Sedayeh Payeh Ab*)

This is how Sepehri looks at the world. In this world, in this faith, in this poetry, is an invitation to listen to a symphony of words, to travel bare and bewildered, to where earth and sky intertwine.

> *I saw light fluttering in a door-less cage.*
> *Ishq, climbing a ladder to heaven.*
> *A woman, pounding light in a mortar...*
> *I saw a beggar going from door to door asking*
> *for lark song...*

> *I saw a train carrying seeds of water lilies and*
> *songs of canaries...*
> *Ishq was visible, waves were visible,*
> *Snow was visible, love was visible.*
>
> From 'Sound of the Footsteps of Water' (*Sedayeh Payeh Ab*)

It is from this vantage point that Sepehri makes his call for compassion, love and justice.

> *One day*
> *I shall come and a message I shall bring.*
> *Into veins I shall pour light*
> *And I shall call out:*
> *You whose baskets are full of sleep!*
> *Apples I have brought, red apples of the sun*
> *I shall come, and to a beggar a jasmine I shall give.*
> *Upon the lovely leper woman a pair of earrings I shall bestow.*
> *To the blind I shall say: Look at the lovely garden!*
> *A peddler I shall become*
> *And up and down the street shall cry:*
> *Dew, dew, dew.*
>
> From 'A Message to Come' (*Peyami Dar Rah*)

Sepehri, enamoured of the world but with his roots deep in Kashan, weaves the two together with the silks and velvets of his native town. Pomegranate blossoms, mud walls, silk and perfume come alive in his poetry, become characters who talk, laugh, become angry, dance and create an outburst of colour, light, happiness and pain. He creates a rainbow of trees, stones, light and water. All this, so that one can look into that mirror-picture he creates, to appreciate one's own beauty and value, the beauty and value of humanity, the beauty and value of nature and the marvel of being. That was the miracle that dawned on him – the miracle he believed in and the miracle he wanted to convey.

Sepehri's poetry is also a world full of colourful secrets and symbols, of wonder and awe for times past; a world full of mythical visions. In his work, the interwoven myths of Iran, India, and China are an invitation to the distant past of humanity's childhood. He delves into the most ancient of Iranian and Indian mythology and symbolism to carry his readers to the bright and shining tomorrow of mankind. On that road he sweeps us along until something bursts open inside, and we become not only more appealing, but bare and visible to ourselves. He invites us to the childhood of a world of light, rain and mirrors, mirror facing mirror, carrying one to infinity. It is the mystic's enraptured outlook on the world of being.

His poetry conveys a broad spectrum of the relationship of humanity to nature, full of song, play, words, trees, seas, stones, in a passionate dance, arms flung wide, entranced. His words are full of clarity, compassion and nobility, like the human beings he describes. This is a poet completely fascinated by and committed to *ishq*. It is the shining jewel of his poetic works, reflected in his *ishq* for humanity, for nature, for existence. He is unquestioning as to where we come from, what language we speak, what our religion is. For Sepehri, *ishq* knows no frontiers and recognises no borders until, like the most brilliant of humanity's achievements in its evolution towards real freedom, true independence and nobility, it takes its place in the forefront of the history of the century. To arrive at that goal we have to wash our eyes, look in a different way. He says, 'Let us stand under the rain and with new eyes look at our world':

Walk in the rain
Take memory and thought under the rain
Meet friends in the rain.
Sleep with a woman under the rain.
Play in the rain
Write, talk, plant water lilies in the rain.
From 'Sound of the Footsteps of Water' (*Sedayeh Payeh Ab*)

This poetry is a new and colourful approach to the continuous innovation and evolution of man and being. In this sense it is a form of painting. His words – like colour, light and lines – are in motion, travelling, dancing, mixing and merging, producing simple, beautiful and visionary images before our eyes. These images cannot be reiterated, like a river, a human being, a vision. Trees, light, rivers and waves fill his poetry.

> ... I am full of lanterns,
> Full of light and sand,
> Full of trees and evergreens
> Full of roads, bridges, rivers
> Full of the shade of a leaf in the water:
> How lonely I am inside.
> From 'Light, Flowers, Water and I' (*Rowshani, Man, Gol, Ab*)

But it is in this loneliness that the overflowing occurs. It is in the silence that he hears. In darkness that he sees. He sees, hears, absorbs light, climbs to the top of the mountain, runs to the end of the plain and calls:

> Life is not empty,
> Kindness exists, apples exist, faith exists
> Yes,
> As long as poppies bloom, life must be lived.
> From 'Golestaneh' (*Dar Golestaneh*)

Sepehri's world culminates in a tomorrow and a future for humankind that lies behind Heechestan – the land of 'no thingness'. To arrive there:

> A boat I shall build
> In the water I shall launch it...
> Beyond the seas lies a city...
> From 'Beyond the Seas' (*Poshteh Daryaha*)

The poetry of Sohrab Sepehri is the language of the times. It is a compassionate, luminous fire that in the dark nights of loneliness grants us light and clarity, calling humanity towards a tomorrow full of hope. Let us close tired eyes and drink the soft melodies of these bubbling springs of poetry. Naked and drunk, let us stand under the waterfall of light and brightness. Listen. Look. Birds full of ardour, words all blue, take flight from his lines and settle on your shoulders and hands, pecking at the fragments of light and *ishq* they find there. Look, for we are nothing but a gaze!

Tonight,
In a strange dream,
The road towards words
Will be opened.
The wind will have something to say.
An apple will fall....
...
Tonight
The stem of significance
Shall be shaken by the breath of the Friend.
Bewilderment shall fly away.
...
Inside the word 'morning'
Morning will break.
From 'Till the End in Audience' (*Ta Enteha Hozour*)

The smell of departure is in the air.
My pillow is full of the song of swallows' feathers.
...
Tonight I must go
And travel in a direction
Where epic trees can be seen...
...
My shoes, where are my shoes?
From 'The Initial Call' (*Nedayeh Aghaz*)

Suddenly I was pulled away from earth, delivered, reaching up into the unknown, unheard-of spheres of the sky. Unbound, I arrived at the star that was Sohrab Sepehri. Ever since, I have been unable to walk away from the spell he wove around me. Like a shadow in water, like a child in a mirror, like dawn at the window, a star within a star, a *heech* in Heechestan.

Mahmood Kavir

From Book I

The Death of Colour

(Margeh Rang)

In the Pitch Black of Night (*Dar Ghireh Shab*)

For a long time now, in this loneliness
The colour of silence sits upon my lips.
A distant cry calls me,
But my feet are in the pitch black of night.

Not a single chink in this darkness:
Walls, doors, held fast together.
If a shadow slips and stumbles on the floor
It's the image of an illusion, from fetters freed.

Strange the times
In this corner of stagnant air,
Where everywhere people's breath is bated
And all joy is dead.

Night's bewitching hand
Slams the door – in my face and that of sorrow.
No matter how hard I try,
It only mocks me.

All that I designed in daytime,
Night came and smeared with smoke.
All that I imagined at night,
Day came and erased outright.

For a long time now, everyone, like me,
Has the colour of silence upon their lips.
There is no movement in this darkness:
Hands, feet, in the pitch black of night.

Smoke is Rising (*Dood Meekheezad*)

Smoke is rising from my place of retreat.
When will someone know of my corner of devastation?
With my inner desolation I have much to say.
When will my endless fable end?

I left the lap of night
To cling to the tresses of dawn.
From the shore I flung myself into the water,
Not knowing the depth of the sea.

The design of defeat writ on the walls.
Colour was no longer seen hereabouts.
From deep within, day and night,
Eyes weave visions of hope.

As soon as I stepped in here
From the caravan's bells I broke free.
Though I burn in this heart-consuming fire,
To this burning I am committed.

Darkness draws away from the rooftops:
Morning laughs on its way to my town.
Smoke still rises from my retreat.
With my inner desolation I have much to say.

Dawn (*Sepeedeh*)

In the distance,
A swan, suddenly woken from its sleep,
Washes away indigo dust from feathers white.

The riverbank
Overflows with whispering waves,
On a bed of white.

Light and shadow intermingle.
Gliding through a heap of soot,
A glow-worm, shines in a fire, all white.

In step with the delicate dance of the reed bed,
The marshland opens wet eyes of white.

There is a streak of light upon the darkness:
Upon ebony you'd think shines white gold – white.

The wall of shadows is devastated.
Upon the distant sky, a vision's hand
Has built a palatial mansion, of marble white.

The Riddle Bird (*Morgheh Moamma*)

For ever so long, on a branch of this willow
Sits a bird, the colour of a riddle.
Attuned to him no sound, no colour.
Totally alone, like me, in this land.

Though inwardly ever full of tumult,
In appearance, silent he remains.
Should this pregnant silence ever break,
It will shake the order of the day.

No way out, though the bird is in full song,
Its silent form a telling voice.
The seconds pass before his wakeful eyes,
His form, though, the shadow-light of dreams.

Feathers and wings grown from above and below.
Life, a distant dream: waves of a mirage.
His shadow congealed along the length of the wall,
Wall and shadow draped in a dream.

Eyes fixed on imaginary designs.
In them no empty desires.
Since a bond ties me to his silence,
His inner eye seeks no words with others.

The bird's tale comes straight from the heart:
What fails to arrive is idle fancy.
His are ties with cities lost:
The riddle bird is a stranger in this land.

A Light at the Heart of Night (*Roshaneh Shab*)

Fire is alight at the heart of night
And beyond its smoke,
A scene of distant desolation.
If a grating sound be heard,
It's dry bones rattling in a grave.

My stove has been cold for ever so long,
My lamp, deprived of light.

Sleep carried the watchman away.
Soundless, someone came through the door.
In the darkness, he lit a fire,
Unaware though
That in the watching, a look was consumed.

Though I know that eyes have paths to the spell of night,
Yet from the bright openings in a happy dream
I see the fire alight at the heart of night.

Mirage (*Sarab*)

The sun, and the desert so vast!
No grass, no trees here seen,
But for the crowing of ravens,
A valley deserted of all sound.

In the distance, behind a curtain of dust
A black point flickers from afar:
If the eye strains forward, it will see
Someone, plodding a path.

Body broken by fatigue.
Head and face covered with dust.
Throat parched with thirst.
Bare, thorn-cut, bleeding feet.

With each step forward, at horizon's feet
A sea of water he finds.
A few steps on and he thinks,
'It is only a dream.'

Towards Sunset (*Roo beh Ghorub*)

Sunset's crimson falls,
Highlighting the stones in places.
The mountain is silent,
The river roars.
In the midst of the plain remains
A mound of darkest blue.

Shadow blends with shadow.
Stones bond with stones.
A worn-out day is on its way.
Beguiling to its eyes, the notion of
Sadness in search of a smile.

On high turrets, the owl hoots
The vultures, ominous,
One by one land from the air,
Seeking carrion left on the plain,
Sharp beaks pluck eyes out of sockets
Below the forehead, remain
Two dark, hollow holes.

Darkness approaches.
Silent falls the plain.
The colourful story of the day
Moves towards completion.

Branches dejected,
Stones depressed,
River moaning, owl hooting,
Sadness entwined with sunset colours.
From my lips a cold story flows:
My heart sad in sunset's tightness.

Sorrowful Sadness (*Ghami Ghamnak*)

A cold night and I, dejected.
Tired feet, and a long road ahead.
Darkness, and a lamp gone dead.

Alone, I walk down the road:
Far removed from one and all.
A shadow passed over the wall,
Adding sorrow to my sadness.

The thought of darkness and this desolation
Came silently and unannounced,
In secret, to weave stories with my heart.

With no colour to tell me:
'Patience, dawn is at hand.'
Each moment this wail rises from my heart:
'Heavens, how dark is the night!'

Where a smile to cheer my heart?
A drop to throw into the sea?
A rock to which I could cling?

This is why the night is dank.
Others too are sad at heart,
My sadness, though, is sorrowful sadness.

Ruin (*Kharab*)

My eyes grew old peering into the distance,
Till finally they believed me that life
Was an imaginary colour upon the face of a dream.

I entrusted my heart to separation's pain, but to what avail?
My night of splendour ended
With the morning of recrimination.

My eyes never drank from this defeat-laden life.
This house was built on foundations of water.

With a parched throat only, I plied the path.
My feet stung by desert thorns.
If anyone, helpfully, held my hand,
It was but a mirage, another illusion.

The good things of life were fleeting moments:
With my heart full of pain, Night had a secret slowness,
With Day's work though, a surge of liveliness.

Talk of mortality cast a pall upon my life.
In my heart, the call of happiness was muted, since from the start
The image of the owl was this ruin's only adornment.

One Who Revives (*Jan Gerefteh*)

Tonight, a tune burst open the grave of my mind,
Poured life into the veins of one who was dead,
Rose from among the shadows and the light,
Shouting at me: 'Thinking me dead
You entrusted me to the dust of bygone days?
Futile your thoughts,
My very form drives death away.
My destiny is tainted with the venom of bitter moments.
With every opportunity I will assail you,
And contaminate your joys with pain.
To your imaginings I shall give forms and figurations
That shall make your resolve pale to naught,
That shall mix pain and pleasure
That pour in each of your heartbeats,
Recalling dust-covered images of old.'

The dead thing was tight-lipped and silent,
Eyes flickering at an inauspicious plan.
Pain oozed out of my body,
A tune burst upon my mind.

The Silent Valley (*Darehyeh Khamoush*)

Silence has broken its bonds.
In the corner of a valley, a willow in full splendour stands.
In the twilight-coloured sky
A white cloud passes by.

Silently, through the vein of every leaf, runs the breeze.
Behind every rock sits a fear, in ambush.
From behind a stone, a lizard lifts its head.
Fearful of the silent valley,
Motionless it sits,
Surveying the road with cold, dry, bitter and sorrowful eyes.

Like a snake, a trail winds up the mountainside.
On the trail, a traveller.
Thoughts of the valley, of loneliness
Run fear through his veins.
From every crevice in the mountain
A snake slithers out.
Behind every stone
Angry thorns, daggers drawn.

Evening has flown from the mountain.
Lost to the eye are both trail and traveller.
Full of fanciful fears, a huge sadness
Sits in the rough and rocky landscape.
In the dark valley,
Silence has broken its bonds.

The Death of Colour (*Margeh Rang*)

A colour, on the edge of night,
Wordless, has died.
From faraway places, a bird, all black, has come
From rooftops to sing of the night of defeat.
Joyful and proud, from a recent victory it has come,
This sorrow-worshipping bird.

In that defeat of colour
The chords of every song unravelled.
Alone, the song of that courageous bird
With echoes,
Adorns the ears of this simple silence.

The bird, all black, has come from faraway places
To sit motionless, like a stone,
Upon the roof of the night of defeat.
Its eyes move from side to side
Following the forms of its confused imaginings.
A strange dream troubles it:

> *The flowers of colour spring from the soil of Night.*
> *In perfume-scented streets*
> *The breeze moves no more.*

Every moment, in deceptive hope this sorrow-worshipping bird
Draws new plans, with the help of its beak.

A bond has broken,
A sleep disturbed.
The prevailing outlook
Has erased from memory
The fable that the flowers of colour will reappear.
Wordless, one must pass this bend in the road.
On the edge of this endless night, a colour has died.

Dang... (*Dang...*)

Dang... dang...
In the night of a lifetime
The confused clock of Time repeatedly tolls.
The poisonous thought, that this is just a passing moment
Is imprinted within the veins of my being.
My moment is either full of pleasure
Or mixed with the rust of sorrow.
Yet, since this moment must pass,
If I cry
My tears will serve no purpose,
And if I laugh
My laughter will be of no avail.

Dang... dang...
The moments pass.
For that which goes comes no more.
A story that can never again
Have a beginning.
As if a question that has no answer
Has frozen upon the cold lips of Time.
Hurriedly I leap up
To cling to the wall of that moment in which everything
Is tinted with delight.
What remains of this effort:
The smile of an instant now lost to my eyes,
And the imprint of my fingers
Upon that moment's form.

Dang...
An opportunity lost.
A story ended.
One moment must follow another
For continuity to come alive in the mind.
Continuity that pours poison in my veins
Depriving me of the idea of the here and now,
And from far and distant places
Binds me to thoughts of decay and decline.

One scene passes,
Another comes forward:
One image after another,
One colour merges into another.
In the night of a lifetime
The confused clock of Time repeatedly tolls:
Dang... dang...
Dang...

A Man and the Sea (*Darya wa Mard*)

Alone, along the shore,
Walks a man.
At his feet
The sea, surging, clamouring.
The night, giddy with the heaving waves.
The wind, terrifying,
Turns toward the beach and into the eyes of the man,
Darkening both the design and colour of danger,
As if saying,
'Hey, where are you going, man? Where?'
The man goes his way.
The vagrant wind
Calls out again: 'Where are you going man? Where?'
The man goes his way,
As does the wind…

Daunting breakers
Keep arriving,
Overflowing with arrogance, aggression.
One such, full of dread,
Sweeps across the shore and swallows
A shadow, stripped of all patience by the night.

The sea, surging, clamouring.
The night, giddy with the heaving waves.
The wind, terrifying,
Turns towards the beach and…

A Happening (*Sargozasht*)

The sea is in uproar.
On the seashore, no one to be seen.
On the dark waters, not even a spot
That could, were it to approach, be a boat.

On the seashore remains
A boat that has suffered the blows of the night.
Its frame, in some strange way,
Drowned in bitter perceptions.
No one arrives
To return it to the sea.
While every heave of water
Speaks to it in secret,
An agitated wave arrives to tell us
The story of a stormy night at sea.

That night, a fisherman had gone
To bring in from the sea
What seemed more like
Fantasies in a dream.

The morning after, when in the water
One wave did not move to beat against another,
Fishermen saw a boat at sea, that told
The story of the bitter night before.
They pulled the boat towards the sleepy shore,
Right where, at this sad moment, it rests.
And nearby,
The sea is in uproar
And from far away, a wave arrives that once more tells
The not very long story
Of a night, a stormy night at sea.

An Image (*Naqsh*)

One dark night
Where no sound mingled with another
And people seemed so far apart,
Someone climbed the rocky mountain
And with bloodied nails
Carved an image on a stone and was seen no more.
Rainwater washed away the blood that had oozed
from his wounds and dried on the rocks.
Storms erased the marks
That his footsteps had left behind.
Whoever you now ask,
His name is no longer remembered,
His story no longer told.

That night
No one came
To tell of the colour that was about to burst.
The mountain, grave, brooding, indifferent.
The wind came, but quietly.
The clouds fluttered, very gently.
But at that instant, when the nails of the Master of Mystery
Reached towards the slab of stone upon which,
in a brief instant, had been carved
An image meant to last till eternity.

Tonight
Wind and rain are both beating down:
The wind, to uproot a stone from its place.
The rain,
To wash away an image from that stone.
Both in earnest
Both in uproar.
But the stone, untroubled, stands upright on the mountain,
Remains steadfast, as if chained with steel.
The years have neither moved nor eroded it.
All this effort – futile.
Even if the mountain fell apart,
The stone, calm and collected would stay in place.
Nor will that image ever erode, carved as it was, in one brief moment,
By someone who climbed the rocky mountain
One dark night.

From Book II

The Life of Dreams

(*Zendehgiyeh Khabha*)

The Wet Lantern (*Fanouseh Kheece*)

Over the grass I have trickled.
I am the sleep-mingled dew of a star
That has seeped over weeds of darkness.
My place was not here.
I hear the wet whisperings of the weeds.
My place was not here.
A lantern
Bathes in the clamorous cradle of the sea.
Where is it going,
This very thirsty, inebriated, sea-worshipping lantern?
On the blue-tiled edge of the distant horizon
My gaze follows the misty dance of fairies.
The whisperings of the night grow in my veins.
Rain, full of the seaweed of inebriation
Drips on the thirsty walls of my soul.
I'm a star that has trickled down.

    From the unseen eye of sin I have trickled:
    A night full of desire,
    The warm body of the horizon, naked.
    White veins, running through the green marble of the grass, whispering.
    Moonlight, descending the indigo coloured stairway of the East.
    Fairies, dancing,
    Blue dresses at one with the colour of the horizon.
    And I, drunk with the whisperings of the night.
    The window of dreams was wide open
    And she, like a breeze, blew in.

Now I lie on the grass
And a breeze passes me by.
The throbbing has turned to ashes.
Those in blue no longer dancing.
The lantern gently moves up and down.

> When she flew out of the window
> Her eyes had lost a dream.
> The street was breathing heavily.
> With what desire the rocks inhaled her scent!

Hurrying lantern!
How long will you glide
Up and down the foamy road, full of song?
The whisperings of the night faded.
The dance of the fairies came to an end.
I wish I had not trickled here!

> When the breeze of her body was lost in the deep darkness of the night
> Leaving the seashore, the lantern set out on its way.

I wish I had not trickled here – in the weed-filled bed of darkness!
The lantern slips away from me.
How can I rise,
Glued as I am to the cold bones of the weeds?
Far from me, the lantern
Bathes in the clamorous cradle of the sea.

The Lotus Flower (*Niloofar*)

I was crossing the frontiers of sleep,
The dark shadow of a lotus flower[1]
Had fallen across this rack and ruin.
What impatient wind
Brought the seed of this lotus flower to the land of my dreams?

Behind the glass doors of dreams and visions,
In the bottomless marshes of the mirrors,
Wherever I had died to a part of myself,
A lotus flower has grown.
You'd say that minute by minute it was flowing into my emptiness
And I, in the resonance of its unfolding,
Minute by minute, was dying to my self.

The roof of the verandah was falling in
And the leaves of the lotus flower had covered every corner.
What impatient wind
Brought the seed of this lotus flower to the land of my dreams?

The lotus flower grew,
Its stems rising from the lowest point of my transparent sleep.
I was dreaming.
When floodwaters of awareness arrived.
In the ruins of my sleep, I opened my eyes:
The lotus flower has permeated my whole life.
It was I who was running through its veins.
Its existence had roots in me.
It was my all.
What impatient wind
Brought the seed of this lotus flower to the land of my dreams?

---

[1] According to Iranian mythology, Being was born of a lotus flower

Journey (*Safar*)

After seconds ever so long,
On the grey tree at my window, a leaf is appearing.
A green breeze shook the sleeping core of my body,
And before
I could put down roots in the sands of dreams,
I set out.

After seconds ever so long,
The shadow of a hand over my being fell.
Its moving fingers woke me,
And before
I could throw the rays of my loneliness
Into the dark depths of my inner self,
I set out.

After seconds ever so long,
Over the frozen marshland of Time a warm glow fell.
An anchor came and poured its swaying into my soul.
And before
I could slide into the swamp of forgetfulness,
I set out.

After seconds ever so long,
An instant passed.
A leaf dropped from the grey tree at my window.
A hand gathered its shadow from my being.
An anchor froze in the marshland of Time.
And before I could open my eyes
I glided into another sleep.

From Book III

Burden of the Sun

(*Awareh Aftab*)

Without Warp and Weft (*Bee Tar o Pood*)

In the wakefulness of moments
My body stumbled by a roaring river.
A shining bird alighted,
Gathered my dazed smile and flew away.
A cloud appeared
And in its transparent haste, drank the mist of my tears away.
A bare and endless breeze arrived,
Disturbed the lines of my face and went its way.
A luminous tree
Into its black roots, swallowed my body where it lay.
A flood arrived,
My footprints it stole away.

A gaze leant over the roaring river:
An image shattered.
An illusion broke away

You Who Are So Close (*Eyye Nazdeek*)

In the most secret of orchards, my hands
have plucked fruits.
So, from my fingertips have no fear, branch
so near.
The restlessness of my hands is not a desire
to despoil, but a thirst for friendship.
The brilliance of fruits! Shine even more.
The desire to pluck withered in the forgetfulness
of my hand.
The most distant water
Sprinkled itself upon my path.
The most hidden of stones
Cast its shade upon my feet.
And I, branch so near!
Have foregone water and leaving the shade,
have gone outside.
I went, discarding my pride on mountain heights
where eagles nest,
And here, with bowed humility, at your feet, I remain.
Bend down, branch so near!

The Mirror Flower (*Golleh Ayeneh*)

The dew rains moonbeams.
The marshland overflows with the blue haze of lotus flowers.
On the ground shines a boundless mirror.
> Boundaries slide off one's hand.
> Where did I glide in my sleep?
> My gaze, perplexed in the quiet of the mirror night.
> No pictures reflected in this marshland.

He, god of the marshland, his voice resounding in the haze of distant valleys:

> 'You wind-blown, anxious ones!
> Shake off the dust of sleep.
> One dark seed remains hidden in the lowlands.
> In the soil of the mirror hide that seed.

Throwing off the web of sleep, the wind-blown, anxious ones
Plant the seed in the brittle, dry soil of the mirror.'
God of the marshland calls into the green bowl of silence:

> 'Thirst will burn this dark seed.
> With your warm tears, satiate the soil of the mirror.'

With silvery hands, *houris* of the spring
Brush away the smoke of sleep from crystal-clear eyes.
Clouds in the eyes of the *houris* of the spring rain:

> The warp and weft of the earth trembles to its core.
> The cold breeze of consciousness blows upon me.
> Lotus flower, God of the marshland!
> Where is the silvery key of the door of wakefulness?

In the dark of the night, voices of the *houris* of the spring drift:

You have stepped into an enchanted land,
Your eyes overflowing with misty images!
Open your tightly closed doors
For hidden veils to come alive in the dance of an
intoxicating perfume.

Houris of the spring! Wash away from my sight the binding spell.
You wind-blown, anxious ones!
Shake off the leaves of illusion from my branches.

Houris and anxious ones, in one voice:

>   He, from perfumed openings
>   Upon the soil of distant moments, sees a kindred flower.
>   A dark delight sears his gaze.
>   God of the marshland lotus flowers
>   Turn back the restless wayfarer from the road of illusions.

Who casts spells upon the fountainhead of sleep?
The hands of Night are fog-tainted.
From the mirror, a flame rises like a wave.
Who is this formless visionary with a body on fire?
God of the marshland lotus flowers!
This beauty I cannot bear!

The *houris* of the spring, under moonlit dust:

>   Your vigil has left you bereft of endurance!
>   The naked branches of your sleep are about to sprout.
>   On a limpid, transparent night
>   It's the sound of the cup of loneliness you hear.
>   Beauty and suffering are its warp and weft.

The Mirror Flower (cont'd)

In the midst of distant valleys a quiet voice echoes:

> It's the sound of the cup of loneliness you hear
> Beauty and suffering are its warp and weft.

My warm, eager looks flow with the river of colour.

> I, in that radiance, was the rain on childhood's silver castle.
> The river of dreams carried away a flower.
> With the rushing water I ran, drunk with beauty.
> My hand, on the border of wakefulness,
> Sinking in the dark mists of hopelessness.
> You, whose heartbeats flew away from the bed of my imagination!
> Far from each other, where were we going, so bewildered?
> We, two shores of a wild tune
> We, two birds of the branch of grief
> We, two unruly waves of the same colour?

The wind-blown anxious ones, from the far corners of the marshland:

> The threads of the design wrap around his hands.
> O cool breeze of consciousness!
> Extend the line of his vision
> From the small, colourful window of wakefulness.

In the depth of the night the *houris* of the spring sang:

> Beams of light split open the rock of night.
> If, under the wild round of the wheel of the sun

> The restless form of the mirror breaks,
> Like a perfume, it will fly away from the land of the lotus flower.
> This formless flower of the mirror
> This splendour of the dew of dreams.

> The small flame seemingly dreams of a hurricane.
> Who makes smoke drift across the face of marble tonight?
> Lotus flower, god of the marshland
> With song filling the bowl of Night to overflowing:

>> Under a leaf conceal the mirror from all eyes.
>> The wind-blown anxious ones
>> With a thousand laps full of leaves,
>> Having travelled endless distances,
>> Can be heard from the frontiers of silence:
>>> The stalks of light grow in the pool of darkness
>>> The spellbound night loses its colour.
>>> The mirror is lost in the fog of forgetfulness.

Following the round of the sun, dust rises from the ashes.
The voices of the *houris* and the wind-blown, anxious ones mingle
With the blue dust of lotus flowers:

> The doors of awareness have opened.
> At the entrance a moment of dread fell away.
> At the edge of the spellbound night, the shadow of hesitation falls apart.
> The doorway of visions drank the haze of light.

The Dust of a Smile (*Ghobareh Labkhand*)

Sunshine radiated from the plants.
I saw her in the dewy plains
Drunk with the grieved desire to see, this friend of the wind,
Hair blown away, cheeks drenched with dew.

We saw a poppy – a smile on the face of the plain –
A reflection on the luminous water thrown.
She, casting sound in the cleft of the wind:
'Its grace mingled with the scent of the earth.'

The river shining bright, she, waves of sound:
'Our eyes dazzled by the river of illusion.'
The scene was lit, she sang darkly:
'The plans have the fog of delusion in hand.'

My eyes fell on her form.
'The calamity of decline is near at hand,' she said.
The plain: A sea of throbbing, of song, of light.
Her dark laughter cast a stark shadow.

Another Realm (*Diyari Deegar*)

Between an instant and earth,
there is no heavily laden stalk of fear.
Fellow traveller! To the eternity of flowers we are linked.
The brightness of your eyes to the safekeeping
of sand and stars bestow:
No signs seeping through the seams
of contemplation.
No signs of fear in this soil of clay
Nor any spectacular signs in the deep blue above.
Sink in bird song:
Distressed fluttering of feathers and wings will
cast no shadow on your face.
In the flight of an eagle
There is no design for falling.
The blackness of a thorn does not intrude
between observer and observed.
Beyond that:
Between a sheaf of wheat and the sun
The dread of a sickle was torn apart.
Between lips and a smile
The dagger of Time disintegrated.

We Are The Shady Bower of Our Tranquillity
(Sayebaneh Aramesheh Ma Mayeem)

In the pursuit of duality, fresh faces faded.
Come, let us take the road of shadow/light.
Stand at the edge of dew, alight on a leaf.
If footsteps we find, let's follow ancient travellers.
Unafraid, let us return and in the courtyard
of days past, quaff the magic potion,
Breathe the scented stock of songs, forget our own faces.
Look from the windows of those other places,
welcome the lure of danger,
Soar over apprehensions.
Let us not cling to the lap of security or means of escape.
Do not make haste, either towards clarity
close by or distant vagueness.
Quell thirst, then go towards the spring.
At dawn, recognise the enemy, then signal the sun.
We are stranded, facing nothing, we are bowing,
facing nothing, so let us not disturb the prayers of the mother.
Let us rise and pray:
    May our lips be the perfumed channels of silence!
Nearby, a night that is futile. Avoid it.
By our side a lifeless root. Pull it up.

Unperturbed, step into the slime,
set the dead-still waters throbbing.
Become fire, turn the reed-bed of agitation to ashes.
Become a drop, set the sea in motion.
And this breeze, waft and waft eternally,
And this reptile, bend and coil, and do it deliberately,
And into this deep pit fall, fall without fear.
Pitch a tent over our heads, for we are the shady
bower of our tranquillity.
We are the vibration of rocks; we are vibrating rocks.
We are the stride of night; we are night striders.
We are flight and await one that flies.
We are bubbling water awaiting the pitcher.
Picking fruits out of season, they picked unripe dreams,
while hesitation rotted from over-ripeness
Come, let us leave the salt marshes of good and evil.
Like a river, a flowing mirror let us be: to a tree,
give a tree for an answer.
Let us constantly create our own two borders,
and every minute, liberate them.
Let us go, let us go, whispering of the absence of borders.

Travelling Companion (*Hamrah*)

Alone, in the lamp-less night I travelled,
My hands empty of the memory of torch-light.
All my stars had headed for darkness.
In my hand, the dry stem of heartbeats tightly clasped.
My moment was full of the ring of bonds, breaking.
Alone I travelled. Do you hear me? Alone.
I had set out from the freshness of the emerald garden
of childhood.
Patiently, the mirrors were waiting to see me.
The doors were in search of my grief-stricken passage.
On and on, I travelled, delving into the depths of myself.
Suddenly, you, from the byways of the moments, between two dark
unknowns, joined me.
The sound of my breathing mingled with the flaming form
of your body:

> May all my heartbeats be yours, you with a face at one
> with night! All my heartbeats!
> I have passed the chill fall of star leaves
> To steal lost flames from your body's sinful lines.

I passed my hand over the entire length of Night.
In the awareness of my fingers the whisperings
of benediction flowed.
I clasped a handful of space.
Star-drops shone in the darkness of my being.
In the end,
In the misty music of that benediction, I lost you.

Between us are distant desert wanderings.
Dark nights, earthen beds of exile, the forgetfulness of fires.
Between us are the thousand and one nights
of seeking and searching.

From Book IV

East of Grief

(*Shargheh Andouh*)

Haay (*Haay*)

You are the fountainhead of growth,
an ocean, the goal of contemplation.
You permeated: watered the garden of the universe, changed it.
Some morning broke,
a bird flew, a branch snapped: darkness is here.
Fell asleep, dreamt: water's radiance in a dream,
a leaf quivering in water.
Death's darkness on this side, loveliness of a leaf on the other,
what is this, what is that? And what of the profusion of Time?

This bursts open, fear is something to be seen.
That passes, dread is a sea.
You are shafts of light, shafts from a *mehrab*, glowing. I am nothing:
an ivy asleep, winding round the hand-rail of my grief.

You are darkness of a flight, a vision with no start, no waves,
no colour, a harmonious sea!

Doubt (*Shakpooy*)

A ripple fell on water, an apple fell to the ground.
One step more. A cricket sang
A commotion: Laughter. A banquet. Cut short.
A sleep climbed up an eye. This pilgrim travelled alone,
travelled without us.
The thread broke: I'm a twist, I'm a turn. The jar broke: I'm water.
This stone, what is its connection with me? That bee, where is
its flight to me?
An image, but where the mirror? This smile, but where the lips?
A wave came, but where the sea?
I smell something, a fragrance. From every side,
'*haay*' came, '*hoo*' came. I left, '*he*' came, '*he*' came.

No to Stone (*Na beh Sang*)

In the river of Time, in the vision of your contemplation we go
My smooth face with your scattered dew I wash.
My feathers? Torn away.
My eye full of promise, with a glance, was refreshed.
    Not this side, I'm on that side.
On that side of a glance I see something, seek something.
I break a stone, a secret to your image I impart.
A leaf fell, to my health: On sorrow I live. A cloud passed,
I am a mountain: I last. I am wind: I seek.
In another field, when the flower of regret blooms, I'll come.
Its scent I'll inhale.

And (Wa)

Yes, we are the buds of a sleep.
- Buds of a sleep? I wonder, will we ever bloom?
- One day, without a leaf moving.
- Here?
- No, in the Valley of Death.
- Darkness, loneliness.
- No, a beautiful retreat.
- Who will come to see us, who will breathe our scent?
- ...
- Scatter on a wind..?
- ...
Another landing?
- ...

Na (*Na*)

Open the door, the wind has come, God's grief it has brought.
Sweep the house, scatter flowers, the messenger has come,
the messenger has come with good news from 'Na'.
Water has come, water has come, and from the plains of the gods,
black flowers it has brought
He came while we slept, and the devil's smile to our lips he brought.
Death has come,
Our perplexity he took away.
For you, fear he brought.
Somewhere, in some land, morning came, a golden apple from a
golden garden it brought.

My Fervour (*Shooramra*)

I am a musical instrument, captivated by song. Hold me close, play me.
On my tar strum a 'No', the road to annihilation play.

I am smoke, circling, sliding, non-existent.

I burn, I burn: A lantern of desire. Turn me and enter into a flower.

I have become a mirror, free of light and shadow. Devil and angel came. Devil and angel I was. In ignorance I existed.

The Quran above my head, the gospels my pillow, the Torah my bed, the Avesta close to my skin, I dream: A Buddha in the water lily of the pool.

Wherever the flowers of benediction grew, I picked them. A bouquet I have. Your prayer niche far away: That high up and I far below.

My speech is perfumed, right? The breeze said, 'Come' and carried me off. Without provision I climbed the mountain of 'Where', picked flowers, ate flowers.

Hubbub in my veins. Sprinkle me with water from your spring. Sprinkle, and with one drop refresh me, my fervour beautify.

Make the wind blow, break the door of speech, the footsteps of sound sweep away.
Blow away the smoke of 'Why' and the waves of 'I' and 'We' and 'You'. From my night build a bridge to the colourless poppy, and from this vision place a flower in my eye, a flower in my eye.

Bodhi (*Bodhi*)

An instant ago the doors had opened.
The garden of annihilation had appeared. Not a leaf, not a branch
The birds of a silent place – this silent, that silent. Silence had become articulate.
What was this open space where with a wolf walked a ewe?
The picture of sound, pale; the picture of supplication, pale.
Had the curtain been drawn?
I had gone, he had gone, without our selves we had become.
Beauty was alone.
Every river a sea,
Every being a Buddha had become.

Something Happened (*Gozaar*)

Once more I have come from the fountainhead of sleep,
a wet jar in hand.
Birds singing. Water lilies opening. I broke the wet jar.
I closed the door
And in the patio of your contemplation, sat.

Until (*Ta*)

Rise up, rise up. Break the line of vision, break the black delusion.

– I have come, I have come. Another wind is blowing,
another scent is in the air.

Over my head another willow, another sun.

– This is not your town, not your town.

You hear the tolling of Time: a drop has fallen. By your side
a shadow ran.
Your town is in higher regions, other valleys.

– I have come, I have come, solid rock is shifting;
trees I can hear, singing.

– This is not your town, not your town.

Why is the wing of the eagle weary, the land for sleep so thirsty?
And why the growing and more growing, a mystery detecting?
Your town has other colours, other soil, other stones.

– I have come, I have come. Neither gate nor door closed.
Devils from all sides departing,
And the gods of all the myths that be.
No talk of worship, no anxious eyes straining.

– This is not your town, not your town.

In their hands the bowl of beauty, on their lips the bitterness
of sagacity.

Your town is in other realms, with other feet you must be walking.

– I have come, I have come. Windows are bursting.

The street forlorn, going nowhere, with neither a '*hay*' or a '*hooy*'.

– This is not your town, not your town,
In silent motion, forms and features in a fog of forgetting.
Your town has a different name. You are not tired. One more step.

– I have come, I have come, doors but passageways for winds of non-existence,
A house freed from self, the bowl of duality broken, the shadow of 'One' on earth, on Time.

– Your town is neither this nor that.

Not until your town is lost, will your town be found.

Till the Flower of Naught (*Ta Golleh Heech*)

We were going – trees so tall – the scene so dark!
Some distance remained between us and the flower of naught.
Death on the slopes – clouds on the mountaintops –
birds on the edge of life.
We sang: 'Without you I was a door to the outside,
a look at the distant horizon and a voice in the desert.
We were going – earth feared us – time rained over our heads.
We laughed: The abyss suddenly awoke
and from the hidden ones a song rang out.
Silently we sat, your eyes by distance filled,
my hands full of loneliness, the land full of sleep.
We slept. They say: 'A hand was picking flowers, in a sleep.'

From Book V

Sound of the Footsteps of Water

(*Sedayeh Payeh Ab*)

An Offering to My Mother's Nights of Silence

Sound of the Footsteps of Water (*Sedayeh Payeh Ab*)

I am from Kashan.
Mine is not a bad life.
I have my daily bread, some intelligence and some taste.
I have a mother, better than the leaves of trees.
Friends better than flowing water.

And a God who is close by:
Among these scented stocks, at the foot of that tall pine tree,
In the awareness of water, in the laws of the plant world.

I am a Moslem.
My Mecca is a red rose.
The plain my prayer rug
A spring my place of prayer, my head on light I lay
I perform my ablutions with the throbbing of the windows.
In my prayers flows the moon, flows a river of colour.
Stones can be seen through my prayers.
The particles of my prayers are crystalline.
I pray
When the wind chants the call from the minaret
of the tallest cypress tree.
I say my prayers after the grass has declared 'God is great',
After the wave has cried 'Rise for prayers'.

My Ka'ba[1] is near some water.
My Ka'ba is under acacia trees.
My Ka'ba, like the breeze, goes from garden to garden,
from town to town.

My black stone is the brightness of a garden.

---

[1] Sacred building in Mecca containing the Black Stone towards which Moslems turn in prayer and where they visit on pilgrimage

I am from Kashan.
A painter by calling:
From time to time I build a cage with colours, to sell to you,
For the song of poppies therein confined
To cheer the heart of your loneliness.
What a fantasy, only a fantasy... I know
My canvas is lifeless.
I know full well – my painter's pond is empty of fish.

I am from Kashan.
My lineage may derive
From a plant in India, from a pot shard from the
soil of Sialk[2]
My lineage may derive from a prostitute in Bukhara.

My father, after two seasonal comings of the swallows,
after two seasons of snow
After two seasons of sleeping on the balcony,
My father died, on the other side of the times.
When my father died the sky was blue.
My mother suddenly sprang from her sleep,
my sister became beautiful.
When my father died policemen were all poets.
The grocer asked: 'How many kilos of melons do you want?'
'How much for a heart at peace?' I asked.

My father painted.
Built *tars* and played them too.
Was also a good calligrapher.

[2] Excavated ruins of an ancient town in Iran

Our garden was on the shadow side of wisdom.
Our garden was where feelings and green grass intertwined.
Our garden was where a look, a cage and a mirror met.
Our garden was an arc maybe, of the green circle of happiness.
That day, in my sleep, I chewed the unripe fruit of God.

I drank water in all simplicity.
Picked mulberries without learning
As soon as a pomegranate cracked open
my hand became a fountain of craving.
As soon as larks sang, my heart burst with delight.

At times, loneliness pressed its face against the windowpane.
Longing came, put its arms round the shoulders of feeling.
Thought was at play.
Living was a continuous shower of happiness,
a plane tree full of starlings.
Life in those days was a row of lights and dolls,
An armful of freedom.
Life in those days was a pool of music.

Step by step, the child travelled the distance
in the street of dragonflies.
I gathered my belongings and fled from the town of visions,
My heart full of the alienation of the dragonfly.

To the banquet of the universe I went:
To the desert of despair,
To the garden of *irfan*,
To the brilliantly illuminated terraces of knowledge.

I ascended the stairs of belief
To the end of the street of doubt
To the refreshing air of detachment
To the drenched night of love.
I was seeking someone at the other end of ishq.
I went, I went till women,
Till the bright light of pleasure,
Till the silence of desire,
Till the reverberating sound of loneliness.

I saw many things on this earth:
I saw a child smelling the moon,
Light fluttering in a doorless cage.
Ishq, climbing a ladder to the roof of heaven.
I saw a woman pounding light in a mortar.
At noon, there was bread at their table, fresh herbs,
a plateful of dew, a hot bowl of affection.
I saw a beggar going from door to door asking for lark song.
A garbage man praying in the direction of a melon skin.

A sheep, eating a kite.
A donkey who understood alfalfa.
In the pasture of advice I saw a cow fully satisfied.
I saw a poet talking to a lily and addressing it as 'Thou'.

I saw a book with words of crystal,
Paper, the quality of spring.
I saw a museum far from things green.
A mosque far from water.
At the pillow of a despairing jurist, a jug brimming with questions.

I saw a mule loaded with composition.
A camel whose load was an empty basket of maxims
and proverbs.
A mystic whose load was *tanana ha ya hoo*.

I saw a train carrying light.
A train carrying jurisprudence (and how very heavy it was).
Another carrying politics (and how very empty it was).
I saw a train carrying water-lily seeds and the songs of canaries.
An airplane, thousands of feet high
And earth visible from its windows:
The crest of a hoopoe,
The spots on a butterfly's wing,
The form of a frog in a pond,
The journey of a fly through the street of loneliness,
The clear desire of a bird flying from a plane tree to the ground.
The coming of age of the sun,
And the beautiful, loving embrace of a doll with morning.

Stairs that climbed to the hothouse of desire.
Stairs that went to the crypt of alcohol.
Stairs that went to laws decreeing the decay of red roses,
To the mathematical perception of life.
Stairs that went to the heights of illumination,
Stairs that went to the heights of divine manifestation.

My mother, down below,
Washed teacups in the memories of seashores.

The city was visible.
Its architectural façade: iron, stone, cement.
The pigeon-free roofs of hundreds of buses.
A flower seller putting his flowers on sale.
A poet, setting up a swing between two jasmine trees.
A boy throwing stones at a school wall.
A child spitting an apricot pit on his father's faded prayer rug.
A goat drinking from the Caspian on the map.

The strap of an article of clothing: an impatient bra.

A cartwheel, longing for a worn-out horse,
A horse, longing for a driver fast asleep,
A driver, longing for death.

Ishq was visible, waves were visible.
Snow was visible, love was visible.
Words were visible.
Water was visible and the reflections of things in water.

The cool shelter of cells in warm blood.
The moist side of life.
Sorrow implicit in human nature.
A season of roving in the street of women.
The scent of loneliness in the street of the season.
The summery hand of a fan could be seen.

The journey of a seed to its flowering.
The journey of a morning glory from this house to that house.

The journey of the moon to a pool.
Snowdrops bursting from the earth.
Young vine branches descending from a wall.
Dew raining upon the span of sleep.
Happiness in flight from the ditch of death.
The passing of an event behind spoken words.

A chink struggling with the longing for light.
One step struggling with the distant sun.
Loneliness struggling with a song.
The beautiful struggle of pears with the emptiness of a basket.
The blood-stained struggle of pomegranates with teeth.
Nazis struggling with coquetry.
A parrot struggling with eloquence.
A forehead struggling with cool compassion.

The attack of tiles in a mosque upon prostration.
The attack of the wind upon ascending soap bubbles.
The attack of massed butterflies upon a project to wipe out insects.
The attack of dragonflies upon a row of pipe layers.
The attack of reed pens upon lead type.
The attack of words upon the jaw of a poet.

The conquest of a century at the hands of a poem.
The conquest of a garden at the hands of a starling.
The conquest of a street at the exchange of two greetings.
The conquest of a city at the hands of wooden horsemen.
The conquest of a feast by two dolls and a ball.

A rattle slain on an afternoon mattress.
A story slain on the way to sleep.

Sorrow slain upon orders of a song.
Moonlight slain upon the orders of neon light.
A willow tree slain at the hands of authorities.
A moody poet slain by a crocus.

The face of the earth was visible:
Law and order flowing in the streets of Greece.
Owls hooting in the hanging gardens.
Wind driving a sheaf of history eastward in the Khyber Pass.
A boat carrying a load of flowers on peaceful lake Negeen.
An eternal light shining in every street in Benares.

I saw people.
I saw cities.
The plains, the mountains.
Water and earth.
Light and darkness.
I saw grass in daylight, I saw grass in darkness.
Creatures in light, creatures in darkness.
People in light, people in darkness I saw.

I am from Kashan, but
Kashan is not my hometown.
My hometown is lost.
I, with patience, with fervour,
Built another house on the other side of night.

In this house I am close to the dewy obscurity of grass.
I hear the garden breathing.

I hear darkness falling off a leaf.
I hear light coughing behind a tree.
The sneezing of water from every cleft in the stone.
The song of a swallow from the rooftop of spring.
The clear sounds of the openings and closings
of the windows of loneliness.
The ambiguous sounds of love shedding old skin.
The sweeping desire of a wing for flight.
The cracking of the spirit's self-restraint.
I hear sounds of the footsteps of desire,
And those of the systematic flow of blood through veins.
The dawn-time flapping in a well full of doves.
Heartbeats on Friday nights.
Carnations flowing in thought.
The clear neighing of truth from afar.
I can hear matter blowing in the wind.
And the shoes of faith in the street of yearning.
The sound of rain on the wet eyelids of passion,
On the sorrowful music of the coming of age,
On the songs of pomegranate orchards,
And in the night, the shattering of the bottle of happiness.
The tearing to bits of the paper of beauty,
The wind, filling and emptying the bowl of exile.

I am close to earth's beginnings.
I feel the pulse of flowers.
I know the predestined wet fate of water, the green habits of a tree.

My spirit flows towards the new side of things.
It is young.

Sometimes, sheer enthusiasm makes my spirit cough.
It is idle:
It counts raindrops in the seams of the bricks.
Sometimes, like stones by the roadside, it has a reality.
I have not seen enmity between two pine trees.
I have not seen a willow tree sell its shade to the ground.
An elm tree offers its branches to ravens free of charge.

Wherever there is a leaf, my fervour unfolds.
A poppy plant has bathed me in the flow of being.

Like the wings of an insect, I know the weight of dawn.
Like a flowerpot, I listen to the music of growth.
Like a basket of fruits, I am in a rush to ripen.
Like a wine tavern, I am at the edge of indolence.
Like a house by the sea, I fear the eternal ebb and tide.

All the sun you may desire, all the unity you may desire,
all the intensity you may desire.

An apple makes me happy,
As does the scent of camomile.
I have a pure, contented attachment to a mirror
I do not laugh if a balloon bursts,
Nor do I laugh if some ideology divides the moon in two.
I recognise the sound of quail feathers,
The colour of the underside of a crane,
footprints of a mountain goat.
I know full well where rhubarb grows,

When starlings come, when a partridge calls,
when a falcon dies,
What the moon is in the dream of the wilderness,
Death in the stem of entreaty.
The taste of happiness of lovers united.

Life is a happy ritual.
Life has wings as wide as death,
Life has a flight span the size of *ishq*.
Life is not something on the shelf of habit,
to be forgotten by you and me.
Life is the rapture of a hand that plucks.
Life is the first black fig of the season in
summer's astringent mouth.
Life is the experience of a bat in darkness.
Life is the dimension of a tree in the eyes of an insect.
Life is a migrating bird's sense of alienation.
Life is a train-whistle ringing in the sleep of a bridge.
Life is the sight of a garden seen from sealed windows on a plane.
The news of the launch of a missile.
Touching the loneliness of the moon.
Thinking of the scent of flowers on a different planet.

Life is the washing of a plate.

Life is finding a coin in a street canal.
Life is the square root of a mirror.
Life is a flower to the power of eternity.
Life is the multiplication of the earth in our heartbeats.
Life is the uniform and simple geometry of our breath.

Wherever I happen to be, I'll be.
The sky is mine.
Windows, thought, air, love, the earth, are all mine.
What does it matter
If sometimes
The mushrooms of exile appear?

I do not know
Why they say: 'The horse is a noble animal, the dove beautiful.'
But why are there no vultures in anyone's cage?
Why are clover flowers inferior to red poppies?
We must wash our eyes, must see things differently.
We must wash words.
A word must be the wind itself, must be the rain itself.
Fold the umbrellas,
Walk in the rain.
Take memory and thought under the rain.
With everyone in town we must stand in the rain.
Meet friends in the rain.
Find love under the rain.
Sleep with a woman under the rain.
Play in the rain.
Write, talk, plant water lilies, in the rain.
Living is constantly becoming wet.
Living is bathing in the pool of the 'now'.

Let us undress:
Water is only one step ahead.

Let us taste light
Weigh the night of a village, the sleep of a deer.
Fathom the warmth of a stork's nest.

Don't trample the laws of the lawn underfoot.
In the vineyard untie the knots of your taste buds.
If the moon appears, open your mouth,
Don't say that night is a bad thing
Nor that glow worms are unaware of the insights of a garden.

Let us bring baskets,
Take away all this red, all this green.

We shall have bread and cheese in the morning.
Plant a young tree at the turn of every word.
Scatter seeds of silence between two-letter syllables.
Refuse to read a book in which wind does not blow,
Or one where the skin of dew is not wet,
Or one in which cells have no dimensions.
Or wish the fly to disappear from Nature's fingertips
Or want the leopard to leave the door of creation.
To know that if worms did not exist, something would be amiss,
If there were no wild pears, it would be a blow to the tenets of trees.
If there was no death, our hands would be searching for something.
To know that if light did not exist,
the living logic of flight would be overturned.
To know that before the time of corals there was a void in the concept of the seas.

Without asking where we are,
Smell the fresh petunias in the hospital garden.

Do not ask where the fountain of good fortune is
Or why the heart of reality is blue,

Or question forefathers as to the days and nights of their past.

In the past, there is no expanse of life.
In the past, birds do not sing.
In the past, wind does not blow.
In the past, the green windows of pine trees are closed.
In the past, spinning tops are covered with dust.
In the past is the fatigue of history.
In the past, memories of waves cast cold shells
of silence upon the shore.

Let us go to the seashore,
Throw nets in the water,
Catch the freshness of the sea.

Scoop up a handful of sand,
Feel the weight of being.

If we have a fever, not to say harsh words to the moon.
(Sometimes when I have had a fever,
I have seen the moon hang very low,
Hands could reach the ceiling of the realms of angels.
I have seen a goldfinch sing better.
Sometimes a cut in my foot
Has taught me the ups and downs of the earth.
Sometimes, in my sickbed, the size of a flower would be magnified.
Oranges would expand, lamplight become brighter.)
Let us not fear death.
(Death is not the end of the dove.
Death is not the backside of a cricket.

Death flows in the mind of an acacia tree.
Death has a seat in the air and water of happy thoughts.
Death, at the heart of a village night, speaks of morning.
Death enters the mouth with a bunch of grapes.
Death sings in a robin redbreast's throat.
Death is responsible for a butterfly's beautiful colours.
Death, at times, picks sweet basil,
At times drinks vodka,
At times sits in the shade, looking at us
As we all know,
The lungs of pleasure are full of the oxygen of death.)

Let us not close the door on living words of destiny
that we hear from behind walls of sound.

Raise the curtains:
Let feelings have an airing.
Let maturity spend a night under whatever bush it chooses.
Let instinct go out and play,
Take off its shoes and following the seasons, fly from flower to flower.
Allow loneliness to sing a song,
Write something,
Go into the street.

Let us be plain and simple.
Plain and simple, whether at the till of a bank or under a tree.

It is not for us to know the secret of a red rose.
Our task, maybe, is
To swim in the mystery of that rose,

Pitch a tent beyond discernment,
Wash our hands in the rapture of a leaf and sit at table.
To be born in the morning at sunrise.
Put all agitation to flight
On the awareness of space, colour, sound, and windows,
sprinkle flowers, like dew.
Recognise the sky between two letters of 'Being'.
Fill and empty our lungs from Eternity.
Relieve the sparrow's back from its load of learning.
Take back the names we have given to a cloud,
To a plane tree, a mosquito, summer.
Rise to the heights of affection on the wet feet of rain.
Open the doors towards people, light, greenery and insects.

Our work, maybe, is this:
That between the lotus flower and the century
To pursue the song of Truth.

Chenar Village, Kashan
Summer 1964

From Book VI

The Traveller

(*Musafer*)

The Traveller (*Musafer*)

At sunset, amid the wary presence of things,
The eyes of one who waited saw the expanse of Time.
On the table, in the excitement of some early fruits of the season
Flowed the obscure direction of the perception of death.
The wind, on a carpet of comfort,
Diffused garden scents over the smooth edges of life.
The mind,
Holding the glow of flowers like a fan,
Fanned itself.

The traveller
Alighted from the bus.
'What a clear sky!'
The sweep of the road of exile carried him away.

It was sunset.
The vibrating awareness of grass was audible.
The traveller had come and was sitting
On a comfortable seat by the lawn:
'I feel so depressed,
So very, very depressed.
All the way I was thinking of one thing only
And the colours on the mountainside drained my mind.
The path of the road was lost in the grief of the land.
What strange valleys!
And the horse. Do you remember?
It was white,
And like a pure word, on the green silence
of the pasture it grazed.

And then the colourful strangeness of the villages along the road
And then the tunnels.
I feel so depressed
So very, very depressed.
And nothing,
Neither these perfumed moments
darkening on the bitter orange trees,
Nor the chatty friendship in the silence between two petals
of this scented stock,
No, nothing will save me from the rush of emptiness
Coming from every side.
I think
This measured melody of sadness
Will be heard until eternity.'

The traveller's eyes fell on the table:
'What lovely apples!
Life gives rise to loneliness.'
The host asked:
'What is the meaning of "lovely"?'
'Lovely means expressing forms with passion, with *ishq*.
It is *ishq* and *ishq* alone
That makes you feel at home with the warmth of an apple,
And *ishq* and *ishq* alone
That carried me to the sorrowful expanse of the pains
of life and living,
Brought me to the possibility of becoming a bird.'
'What is the antidote of sorrow?'
'Something that has the clear ring of an elixir.'

By now, night had fallen.
The light was on.
They were drinking tea.

'Why are you so depressed? You seem so lonely.'
'And how very lonely!'
'I imagine
You are preoccupied with that hidden vein of colour.'
'Preoccupied? Meaning what?'
'*Asheq*.'
'Think how lonely
A small fish must feel if it is preoccupied with the blue
colour of an endless sea!'
'What a sad and tender thought!'
'Sadness is the secret smile of the gaze of grass
And signals the end of the unity of things.'
'How lucky are plants, in love with light
Which, with outstretched hands, rests on their shoulders.'
'No, union is not possible.
There is always a distance.
Although the roll of the water is a good pillow
For the crisp, pleasant sleep of the lotus flower,
There is always a distance.
One must always be preoccupied,
Otherwise, the perplexed whisperings between two words
Will be forbidden.
Ishq
Is a journey to the pulsating luminosities of the solitude of things.
Ishq
Is the sound of the spaces that…'

'Are drowned in ambiguity.'
'No,
The sounds of the intervening spaces are as shiny as silver
But upon hearing the least thing, become tarnished.
An asheq is always alone
His hand is always in the fragile hands of instants.
He and the instants go to the other side of day.
He and the instants sleep on light.
He and the instants bequeath the best book in the world
To water,
And they know full well
That no fish will ever
Unravel the one thousand and one knots of the river.
In the middle of the night, on the ancient ship of illumination
They will launch upon the waters of providential guidance
And row until the full manifestation of wonder and awe.'
'Your beguiling words help one
Pass through the leafy paths of stories.
And what fresh but sad life flows
In the veins of such a melody!'

The courtyard was lit,
The wind was blowing
The animation of the night flowed in the silence of the two men.

'A room is an unsullied retreat.
What simple scope it has for thought!
I am so depressed,
I have no intention of sleeping.'
He went to the window

And sat on a soft, upholstered chair.
'I am still travelling.
I imagine
There is a boat upon the waters of the world
And I, travelling on board, have for thousands of years
Been singing the abiding song of ancient mariners
In the ears of the windows of the seasons
As on I row.
Where does this journey take me?
Where will footprints cease
And shoelaces be undone by the delicate fingers of leisure?
Where the destination, the spreading of a rug,
Sitting without a care
And listening to
The washing of a dish at a neighbour's tap?'

'And during what springtime
Will I pause
And the surface of the soul be filled with green leaves?
Wine we must drink
And while young, must travel a shadow of a road.
That is all.'

'In which direction does life lie?
From which side do I reach a hoopoe?
Listen, for all during the journey, these same words
Slammed the windows of sleep against each other.
What was singing in your ears all the way?
Think carefully.
Where is the hidden source of this mysterious melody?

What was it that pressed against your eyelids?
What cheerful, heart-warming rhythm?
The journey was not long:
The passing of the swallows lessened the bulk of Time.
In the discourse of wind and tin roofs
Were signs of the beginning of intelligence.
What happened
At the moment, when at the height of summer
You looked at the tumultuous river of Jajrood,
And allowed starlings to reap your green sleep?
The season was the season of harvest
And with the presence of one starling on the branch
of one cypress tree,
A page was turned in the book of seasons,
And the first line read:
"Life is Eve's moment of colourful heedlessness.'"

As you looked:
Between a cow and grass flowed the memory of wind.

Remembering red mulberries on the skin of the seasons
You looked.
The presence of a greenfinch among the clover
Soothed the scratched face of hurt feelings.

Look, there is always a scratch upon the face of feelings.
Something, as if it were sleep's awareness,
Always arrives, softly, like the footsteps of death, from behind,
And places a hand on our shoulders,
And we, taking the warmth of its bright fingers

For a wholesome poison,
Copiously drink it then and there.
Do you remember Venice,
On the quiet canal,
In that resounding argument between land and water
Where time could be seen through the prism?
Did the movement of the gondola nudge your brain?
The dust of habit always accompanies contemplation.
One must always walk with fresh vitality
And blow hard
For the golden face of death to be fully cleaned.

Where is the stone of Rannous?[1]
I come from the neighbourhood of a tree
Upon whose bark the simple hands of exile
Had left a souvenir:
'In my loneliness, this line I wrote as a souvenir.'

Serve the wine.
We must hurry:
I come from a journey in an epic,
And like running water
I know the story of Sohrab and the antidote by heart.

The journey took me to the garden of my childhood
And I stood, until
My heartbeats steadied.

There was the sound of fluttering
And when the door opened
The onslaught of Truth threw me to the ground.

---

[1] A wishing stone in India

And another time, under the sky of the Psalms
On that journey by the river of Babylon, when
I gained consciousness,
The song of the lyre was silent,
And when I listened carefully I heard weeping.
A few restless lyres
Were swinging from the live branches of a willow tree.

And on the way, holy Christian monks
Pointed
In the silent direction of the prophet Jeremiah,
And I, in a loud voice
Read the Book of Ecclesiastes.
Some Lebanese farmers,
Sitting
Under an ancient cedar tree,
Mentally counted
The fruits on their citrus trees.

On that journey, by the roadside, blind Iraqi children
Were looking at
The writing on the Tablet of Hamurabi.[2]

As I travelled,
I received the newspapers of the world.

The voyage was full of flowing.
Due to the clamour of industry, the whole
face of the journey was dark, dejected,
And smelt of grease.

---

[2] A series of tablets, date 1772 BC, inscribed with the law code of the sixth Babylonian King, Hamurabi

On the ground of that journey, empty bottles of drink,
Furrows of natural instincts and shadows of opportunity
Lay next to each other.
From the TB sanatorium, along the route of that journey
Came the sound of coughing.
In the blue sky of the city, prostitutes
Watched
The illuminated tail-streaks of jets in flight
And children ran with their whirligigs.
The street cleaners sang songs,
And well-known poets
Prayed to the emigrating leaves.
The long road of that journey, passing between iron and man
Went in the direction of the hidden core of life,
Attached itself to the wet exile of a river,
The silent glitter of a fish scale,
The familiarity of a melody,
The boundlessness of a colour.

The journey took me to equatorial regions,
And under the shade of that green and impressive Banyan tree
How well I remember
A sentence that came to the summery sphere of memory:
Be wide open, alone, humble and determined.

I come from a dialogue with the sun,
Where is the shade?
But the giddy footsteps of spring are still ongoing
And the hands of the wind still smell of plucking

The sense of touch, that lies behind dust
covering the rapture of an orange
Is still unconscious.
In this colourful tug-of-war, who can tell
Where in the season the weight of my loneliness lies.
The jungle still does not know its own
Innumerable dimensions.
The leaf still
Rides the first letter of the wind…
Humanity is still telling the water something,
And in the conscience of grass the river of an argument flows.
Around the tree,
The fluttering wings of doves tell of the ambiguous
presence of human activity.

Sounds of an uproar approaching.
I am the only one addressed by the winds of the world.
Only to me did the rivers of the world
Teach the pure symbols of effacement,
Only to me.
I am the interpreter of the birds of the Ganges valley.
By the road called Serenat I have explained
The mystical symbolism of the earrings from Tibet
For the bare lobes of the daughters of Benares.
Morning song of the Vedas, on my shoulders place
All the weight of freshness
For I
Am involved in the heat of debate.
And all you olive trees of Palestine,

Your abundant shade address to me,
To this lonely traveller who, from a journey
around Mount Sinai arrives
And who, from the fever of divine speech is aglow and on fire.

But conversation will one day be wiped out
And the highway of the sky
Shall be clarified
By the splendour of sensations radiated by butterflies.
For this elegant anguish what poetry they composed!

But someone is still standing under a tree,
And a rider is still behind the city wall
The weight of the happy dream of victory at Qadisiyeh
On the shoulders of his wet eyelids.
The neighing of his impatient Mongol horses
Still sound from the quiet of clover fields.
On the Spice Road, traders from Yazd
Still faint at the thought of merchandise from India.
And by the Hamoun River you still hear:
'Evil has overtaken the world
A thousand years have passed
No sound of bathing has been heard
And no image of a virgin has appeared in the water.'[3]

Halfway through the journey, on the banks of the Jumna
I sat
Looking at the Taj Mahal reflected in water:
The marbled continuity of elixir-touched moments,
And the progression of the mass of life towards death.
Look, two wide wings

---

[3] In Zoroastrian mythology, at the close of every 1,000-year cycle, a virgin bathing in the Hamoun River will become pregnant and give birth to the awaited saviour

Are travelling towards the edge of the spirit of water.
There are singular sparks at hand.
Come and illuminate the darkness of perceptions.
One sign is enough:
Life is a gentle touch
Upon the slab of Megar.[4]

On the journey of the birds of the Garden of Neshat.[5]
The dust of everyday experience was washed away from my eyes
And I was shown the wholeness of a cypress tree.
Placing the urge to worship
In the care of the luminosity of a moment of ecstasy,
I sat by Lake Tal and fervently said my prayers.

We must cross over,
Join the flow of distant horizons,
And at times, pitch a tent in the vein of a spoken word.
We must cross over
And at times, eat mulberries from the tip of a branch.

I passed by the chanting of love songs.
It was the season of blessings.
Underfoot, numerous pebbles were kicked around.
A woman heard,
Came to the window, looked at the season.
She was young
And her rough peasant hands gently gathered the dew of the moments
From the face of the forebodings of death.
I stopped.
The sun of love songs was high
And I was in charge of the evaporation of dreams

[4] A wishing stone in India
[5] A legendary garden in India

The singular heart beats of the grass, in my mind
I counted:
We imagined
That we had no bounds.
We imagined that inside the epic convulsions of rhubarb[6]
We swam
And a few seconds of oblivion constituted our being.

We were at the stupendous start of grass
When the eye of the woman fell upon me:
'It was the sound of your footsteps. I thought the wind
Was passing over ancient curtains.
Your footsteps, around things
I had heard.'
'Where is the feast of all lines and writings?'
'Look at the undulations, the diffusion of my body.'
'From which side do I arrive at the spacious surface?'
'My extension, all the way to the wetness of the glass
Fill with thirst.'
'Where will life become as precise
As concern over the breaking of a vessel?
Will the warmth of the horse's mouth melt
The secret of how fairy cheese grows?'[7]
'And in the beautiful onrush of hands, one day,
We heard the sound of the plucking of one bunch.'
'And where was it that we sat on nothingness
And in the warmth of an apple washed our hands and faces?'
'The sparks of the impossible arose from existence.'

---

[6] In Iranian mythology, the first man and woman were born from a rhubarb plant

[7] Another name for hibiscus (a friendly, non-toxic flower considered helpful for repelling negative spirits), so-called because its fruit is shaped like a round cheese

'Where will frightful looks be softened
And become more invisible than the path of a death-bound bird?'
'In the dialogue of bodies the course of the white
poplar was so clear!'
'What road will take me to the garden of interludes?'

We must cross over.
I hear the sound of the wind, we must cross over.
I am a traveller, you constant winds!
To the wide-open forms of the leaves take me.
To the fervent childhood of the waters take me.
My shoes, until the perfection of the form of a grape,
Fill with the beautiful flow of humility.
Allow moments, like the endless pigeons
In the white skies of instinct, to soar.
And my chance existence by a tree
Exchange with one pure, lost relationship.
In the breathing of loneliness
The small doors of my awareness bang together.

Set me running after the high-flying kite of that day.
To the quiet retreat of the distant dimensions of life take me.
The presence of a gentle, no-thing *heech*
Show me.

Babol
Spring 1966

From Book VII

Green Mass

(*Hajmeh Sabz*)

Over Eyelids of the Night (*Az Rouyeh Pelke Shab*)

The night was overflowing.
The river, from the foot of the pine trees,
moved into the distance.
The valley, bathed in moonlight; the mountain,
so luminous that God was visible.

On the heights, you and I.
Distances lost, surfaces washed, eyes more tender than the night.
You were offering me the green stem of a message.
With your breath, the earthenware of communion slowly cracking,
Our heartbeats falling on stones.
An ancient wine made summer sands flow in our veins.
The lustre of moonlight adorned you.
You, so wondrous, so free, so worthy of the earth.

The green opportunity of life at one with cool mountain air.
Shadows returning,
But still, in the path of the breeze,
Mint stalks quivered,
And raptures collided.

Light, Flowers, Water and I (*Rowshani, Man, Gol, Ab*)

No cloud.
No breeze.
I sit by the pool:
Fish darting round, light, flowers, water and I.
The purity of a cluster of life.

My mother picks sweet basil.
Bread, basil and cheese, a cloudless sky, wet petunias.
Salvation at hand, amongst flowers in the courtyard.

Light in a copper bowl, what cascading caresses.
A ladder against a high wall brings morning down to earth.
Everything hidden behind a smile.
My face, seen in an opening in the wall of Time.
There are things I do not know,
But I know if I uproot anything green I shall die.
I rise to the heights full of wings and feathers,
See my way in the dark, am full of lanterns,
Full of light and sand, full of trees,
Full of roads, rivers, bridges, waves,
Full of the shade of a leaf in water:
How lonely I am, inside.

A Message to Come (*Peyami Dar Rah*)

One day
I shall come and a message I shall bring.
I shall pour light into veins.
I shall call out: 'You with baskets so full of sleep.
Apples I have brought, red apples of the sun!'

I shall come and to a beggar, a jasmine I shall give.
Upon the lovely leper woman another pair of earrings I shall bestow.
To the blind I shall say: 'Look at the lovely garden!'
A peddler I shall become and up and down the streets shall cry:
'Dew, dew, dew.'
A passerby shall say: 'What a dark night it is.'
The Milky Way I shall give him.
On the bridge is a legless girl.
The stars of Ursula Major round her neck I'll place.
All insults from lips I shall remove.
All walls I shall tear down.
Highwaymen I shall tell: 'A caravan has come laden with smiles!'
Clouds I shall tear apart.
Eyes with the sun I shall entwine, hearts with *ishq*,
shadows with water, branches with the wind.
The chirping of crickets I shall link to the sleep of a child.
Kites I shall fly.
Flowers I shall water.

I shall come and before horses and cows
the green grass of endearment I shall spread.
Pails of dew for thirsty mares I shall bring.
I shall brush away the flies on an aged donkey in the street.
I shall come and on top of every wall a carnation I shall plant.
At every window a poem I shall recite.
To every crow a pine tree I shall give.

Shall tell the snake: 'What magnificence has the frog!'
Reconciliation I shall bring.
Friends I shall make.
For walks I shall go.
Light I shall eat.
I shall love.

Plain Coloured (*Sadeh Rang*)

The sky, more blue.
Water, more blue.
I'm in the courtyard, Ra'na by the pool.

Ra'na is washing clothes.
The leaves are falling.
In the morning my mother said: It's a depressing season.
I told her: Life is an apple, you must bite it with its skin.

The woman next door, at her window, crochets, reads.
I read the Vedas. Sometimes
I sketch a stone, a bird, a cloud.

Pure sunshine.
The starlings have come.
Nasturtiums have just appeared.
As I seed a pomegranate I say to myself:
If only the seeds of people's hearts were visible.
A drop of pomegranate juice flies into my eye: I shed tears
My mother laughs,
So does Ra'na.

Water (*Ab*)

Let's not muddy the water.
Downstream, a pigeon appears to be drinking.
Maybe, in a distant thicket, a goldfinch is washing its feathers,
Or, in some village, a jug is being filled.

Let's not muddy the water.
Maybe it flows by the foot of a silver poplar, to wash away the sadness of some heart.
Maybe the hand of a dervish is dipping his dry bread in it.

A beautiful woman has come to the river.
Let's not muddy the water,
The beautiful face has doubled in number.

How delicious is this water!
How clear this river!
What clarity and purity people upstream must enjoy!
May their springs always be in full flow, their cows full of milk!
I have not seen their village,
God's footsteps must be by their mud walls.
There, moonlight lights up the span of speech.

In the village upriver the mud walls must be low.
Its people know what kind of flowers poppies are.
Surely, there, blue is blue.
When a bud opens, people are aware of it.
What a village it must be!
May their orchard paths be full of music!
People at the source understand water.
They do not muddy it. We too –
Let's not muddy the water.

Golestaneh (*Dar Golestaneh*)

Spacious plains, how very open!
Mountains, how very high!
What a scent of grass in Golestaneh!
I, in this village, am in search of something:
A dream, maybe,
A ray of light, a handful of sand, a smile.

Behind the poplar trees
Innocent heedlessness was calling me.

By a reed bed I waited, a wind was blowing; I listened.
Who was talking to me?
A lizard slithered by.
I set out.
A clover field by the roadside,
A cucumber patch, colourful bushes
And the forgetfulness of the earth.

By a stream
I slipped off my slippers and sat, my feet in water.
How alive I am today,
My whole body throbs with life!
I hope no grief looms behind the mountain.
Who lurks behind the trees?
No one. In the field, a cow grazes.
High noon in summer.
The shadows know what a summer this is.
Spotless shadows,
A corner bright and clean.
Children of feeling! The place to play is here.
Life if not empty:
Kindness exists, apples exist, faith exists.
Yes,
As long as poppies bloom, life must be lived.

In my heart there is something like a blaze of light,
like a sleep at dawn,
And I so restless that I long
To run to the end of the plain, to climb to the top of the mountain.
In the distance, a voice. Who calls me?

Lonely Exile (*Ghorbat*)

The moon, high above the village,
The villagers, asleep.
On the terrace, I smell the pull of loneliness. It hangs heavy.
Lights still on in the neighbour's garden.
My light is out.
The moon shines on a plateful of cucumbers,
on the rim of the water jug.

Frogs croak.
At times, an owl hoots.

The mountain is so near: behind the ash and maple trees.
The plain is visible,
Not so the stones, nor the flowering bushes.
Shadows, like the loneliness of water,
like the song of God, visible in the distance.

It must be midnight.
That is Ursula Major – two hand spans above the roof.
The sky is blue no more. It was blue in the daytime.

Tomorrow I must remember to go to Hassan's orchard
to buy plums and apricots.
Tomorrow I must remember to sketch the goats by
the slaughterhouse.
To sketch the brooms, reflected in water.
I must remember to rescue butterflies that fall in the water.
I must remember not to do anything that
clashes with the order of the earth.
Tomorrow I must also remember to wash my towel by a stream.
I must also remember that I am alone.

Above loneliness hangs the moon.

The Fish Were Saying (*Peyghameh Maheeha*)

I had gone to the pond
Perchance to see the reflection of my loneliness in the water.
There was no water in the pond.
The fish were saying:
'It is not the fault of the trees at all.
It was a hot summer's noon
The bright water-youth sat by the edge of the pond
When the sun-eagle came and scooped him up – for ever.

Who cares if we are deprived of oxygen,
Or the shine never returns to our scales?
But that resplendent sun,
An image of that red carnation in the water,
Whose heart throbbed behind folds of feigned
indifference whenever the wind blew,
That was our eye.
A doorway to a confession of faith in Paradise.

If you see God in the heartbeat of the garden, make an effort
And say that the fish have no water in their pond.'

The wind had a question regarding the plane trees.
I had a question regarding God.

Where is the House of the Friend? (*Neshani*)

'Where is the house of the Friend?'
the horseman asked at dawn.
The sky paused briefly.
A passer-by bestowed the beam of light he held between
his lips upon the darkness of the sands,
And pointing to a silver poplar, said:

'Before you reach that tree,
There is an orchard path greener than the sleep of God
Where *ishq* is as blue as the feathers of friendship.
Go to the end of that path, which extends all the way to maturity,
Then turn in the direction of the flower of loneliness.
Two paces before reaching the flower
You will stop at the eternal fountain of the myths of the earth.
A cold fear will grip you.
In the flowing intimacy of space you will hear rustling:
You will see a child
Who has climbed a tall pine tree
to remove chicks from the nest of Light.
From him you shall ask,
'Where is the house of the Friend?'

An Oasis Within an Instant (*Waheyi dar Lahzeh*)

If you come in search of me,
I am beyond the realm of Heechestan.[1]
Beyond Heechestan is a place.
Beyond Heechestan, the veins of air are full
of dandelion seeds in flight,
Messengers from the full flowering of the furthest clumps of earth.
On the sands are hoof prints, left by handsome
horsemen who, in the morning,
Climbed the hill that poppies ascended.
Beyond Heechestan the span of supplication is open wide:
Whenever a hint of thirst runs in the depths of a leaf,
The alarm bells of rain ring out.
Here one is alone
In this loneliness, the shade of an elm tree flows till eternity.

If you come in search of me
Come softly, come quietly,
Lest the fragile porcelain of my loneliness cracks.

[1] The land of *heech* (no-thingness) – a realm beyond description

Beyond the Seas (*Poshteh Daryaha*)

A boat I shall build,
In the water I shall launch it.
Far behind I shall leave this strange land
Where no one exists to awaken heroes
In the grove of *ishq*.

In a boat empty of nets,
A heart free from desire for pearls
I shall row and row
Free from attachment to things blue
And from mermaids who raise their heads from the water,
And in the glow of fishermen's loneliness
Cast spells from the tips of their tresses.

I shall row and row.
Again and again I shall say:
One must get away, far away.
Men in that city were devoid of myths.
Women in that city devoid of the luscious appeal of a bunch of grapes.
Nowhere in large halls did mirrors reflect exuberance.
Not even a puddle reflected a torch held aloft.
One must get away, far away.
Night has sung its song,
It's the turn of the windows now.

I shall row and row.
Again and again I shall repeat:

Beyond the seas lies a city
Where windows open onto manifestations of the divine.
On rooftops sit pigeons with eyes on the fountain of
human intelligence.

In that city, every ten-year-old has a branch of learning in hand.
The townspeople regard a mud wall
As they regard a flame or a velvety sleep.
Earth hears the music of your feelings,
And in the wind you hear the fluttering of mythical bird-wings.

Beyond the seas lies a city
Where the size of the sun equals the eyes of those who rise at dawn,
Where poets are beneficiaries of water, wisdom, light.

Beyond the seas lies a city!
I must build a boat.

Heartbeat of a Friend's Shadow (*Tapeshe Sayehyeh Doust*)

The village lay some distance away, darkly outlined
Our eyes, full of local legends, evoked the moon.
Night was very close.

We were passing through streaks of mud, now dry on the road,
Ears overflowing with the chatter of open green fields,
Backs loaded with the reverberations of distant cities,
The harsh reality of the land flowing underfoot.

In our ruminations the taste of tranquillity swayed from side to side.
Our shoes, which had prophetic qualities,
with a breeze ripped us off the earth.
On its own shoulder, our walking stick carried eternal spring.
At every turn of thought we each had the whole expanse of the sky.
Each movement of our hands sang with the beating of
dawn-enraptured wings.
Our pockets full of the chirping of childhood mornings.
We were a band of enamoured pilgrims, and our road
Passing by villages familiar with detachment,
Went on toward boundless clarity.

Over a pool, heads bent down of their own accord:
On our faces, night was evaporating,
The voice of the friend reached the ear of the friend.

Songs of a Visit (*Sedayeh Deedar*)

With a basket, I went to the market one morning.
The fruits were singing.
The fruits were singing in the sun.
On the trays, life dreamt of an eternal extension
in the perfection of their skin.
The agitation of the orchards was clear in
the shadow of each fruit.
At times, something unknown swam in the
shining glow of the quince.
Every pomegranate extended its colour to the land of piety.
The vision of our townspeople, unfortunately,
had no resonance when compared to
the radiance of Seville oranges.
I returned home. My mother asked:
'Did you buy any fruits from the market?'
'How could countless fruits be placed in this one basket?'
'I told you to buy three kilos of good
pomegranates from the market.'
'I examined a pomegranate.
It extended far beyond the confines of this basket.'
'Good for you! So what of today's lunch…'

At noon, from the mirrors, reflections of the quince
travelled to the remotest corners of life and living.

A Good Night of Loneliness (*Shabeh Tanhayeh Khoob*)

Listen, the most faraway bird in the world is singing.
The night serene, open and flowing.
Geraniums
And the noisiest branch of the season, hear the moon.

Steps in front of the building,
A lantern in hand
And at the disposal of the breeze,

Listen. From far, the road summons your footsteps.
Your eyes are not meant to bedeck darkness.
Shake open your eyes, put on your shoes and come
To a place where the moon's crest will bestow
awareness on your fingers,
And for a time, on a lump of clay, will sit with you
While the psalms of the night, like a song, will entrance you.

There a pious man will tell you:
Nothing equals arriving at a vantage point energised
by the experience of *ishq*.

Feathers of a Song (*Parhayeh Zamzameh*)

There is time yet for the snow on the ground to melt.
Time yet for the folding of water lilies.
The tree is unfinished.
Still under the snow the desire of paper to float in the wind
The fresh brilliance of insect eyes,
And a frog's head rising from the horizon of the awareness of life.

There is time yet for our trays to be filled with talk of *sambousek*
and *Nowruz*.
In this air where there is no sound of growth in a stem
Or the song of a feather arriving from the lyric land of snow,
I long for the sound of birdsong.
There is time yet for the bird of spring to break into delirious song.
So what am I to do?
I, who in a season deprived of chirping,
Long for the sound of birdsong.

It is best that I get up,
Pick up my colours
And on my loneliness paint the picture of a bird.

The Sura of Contemplation (*Sourehyeh Tamasha*)

By contemplation I swear
And by the beginning of speech
By the flight of a dove from the mind
A word is in the cage.

My words were as luminous as the meadow.
I told them:
A sun is on your doorstep
If you open the door, it will shine on your actions.

I also told them:
Stone is not the adornment of the mountain
Just as metal is not the embellishment of an axe.
In the palm of the earth is an unseen jewel
By whose radiance all the prophets were dazzled.
Seek that jewel.
Take moments to the pasture of prophecy.

To them I gave the good news of the coming of the herald,
The nearness of day and the abundance of colour,
The resonance of the red rose behind a wall of harsh words.
I told them:
He who sees a garden in the memory of wood
His face will eternally remain in the swaying of the grove of fervour.
He who befriends the birds of the air
Will have the most peaceful sleep in the world.
He who gathers light from the fingertips of Time
Will open every closed window with an 'Ah'.

We were under a willow tree
I took a leaf from the branch overhead and said:
Open your eyes, do you want a miracle better than this?
I heard them tell each other:
This is magic! Magic!

On each mountaintop they saw a messenger.
They wrapped themselves in the cloud of denial.
We sent down the wind
To blow away their hats and shame them.
Their houses were full of chrysanthemums.
We closed their eyes.
Barred their hands from reaching the top of the Tree of Knowledge,
Filled their pockets with rituals,
Disturbed their sleep with the clamour of departing mirrors.

A Sun (*Aftabi*)

I hear the sound of water. What, I wonder,
are they washing in the river of loneliness?
The moment's clothes are clean.
In the eighth of January sunshine
The resonance of snow, a string of things to see,
the drops of Time.
Freshness sits on bricks, on the bones of day.
What do we desire?
Seasonal mist surrounds our words.
The mouth is the greenhouse of thought.

In their streets they dream of your travels.
In distant villages birds congratulate each
other because of your existence.

Why don't people know
That nasturtiums are not a simple thing?
Don't know that the sparkle of yesterday's seashore
shines today in the eyes of a lark?
Why don't people know
That in the flowers of the impossible the weather is cold?

Stirrings of the Word 'Life' (*Jumbesheh Wajeyeh Zeest*)

Behind the pine forest, snow.
Snow and a flock of ravens.
Streets spell alienation.
Wind, song, traveller and a faint desire for sleep
A branch of morning glory, arrival, a courtyard.

I, homesick, and this wet windowpane
On which I write – and this space.
I write, two walls, and a few birds.

Someone is depressed.
Someone knits.
Someone counts,
Someone sings.

Life means: a starling flying
Why were you unhappy?
Objects of delight are not rare: for example this sun,
The child of day after tomorrow,
Next week's pigeon.

Someone died last night,
But bread is still good,
Water still flows downhill and horses drink it.

Drops, running,
Snow, on the shoulder of silence,
Time, on the spine of a jasmine flower.

The Illuminated Page of Time (*Waraqueyeh Roshaneh Waqt*)

The onslaught of light shook the panes of the door.
It was morning, the sun shining.
We drank tea at the verdant freshness of the table.

At nine o'clock the clouds came, the fence was wet.
My brief moments were hidden under the nasturtiums.
A doll was on the other side of the rain.

The clouds passed.
A clear sky, one bird, one flight.
Where are my enemies?
I was thinking:
In the presence of geraniums, villainy melts away.

I opened the door: a piece of sky fell into my glass.
I drank both water and sky.
My brief moments dreamt silver dreams.
I opened my book under the unseen ceiling of Time.

Midday came.
The aroma of bread was travelling from the sun-kissed
table to the perception of flowers.
The pasture of awareness was in bloom.

My hands swam in the innate colours of being:
I peeled an orange.
The town was visible in the mirror.
Where are my friends?
May their days be orange hued!

Behind the window, all the night you might desire.
In my room, reverberations from the encounter of
my fingers with the heights.
In my room came sounds of the humbling of criteria.
My brief moments mused all the way to the stars.
On my eyes, sleep built a variety of things:
An open space, the sands of song, the footsteps of the Friend…

From Green to Green (*Sabz Beh Sabz*)

I, in this darkness,
Am thinking of a radiant lamb
That will come and graze on the grass of my fatigue.

I, in this darkness,
See the full extent of my outstretched arms
Under a rain
That drenched the first prayers of mankind.

I, in this darkness,
Opened the door to ancient lawns,
To gilded things we saw on the walls of fables.

I, in this darkness,
Saw the roots,
And to the young plant of death, explained the meaning of water.

Forever (*Hameesheh*)

In the afternoon
A few swallows
Flew away from the safety of the pines.
The physical wellbeing of the trees intact.
Pure illumination poured over my shoulders.

Talk, woman of the promised night!
Under these emotional branches of the wind
Entrust my childhood to my hands.
In the midst of these black, endless, forevers
Colourful sister, talk of completion!
Fill my blood with calm consciousness.
My pulse, over the rough body of ishq
Expose.
On the grounds of essence
Walk to the clarity of the mythical garden.
At the first sparkle of fermenting grapes
Talk, houri of original speech.
My sadness, in the distant fountainhead of expressions
Alleviate.
In all the salty sands of indolence
Radiate the voice of water.

Then,
The sweet night-that-was of the eyelids
On the serene and tranquil lawns of consciousness
Spread.

The Initial Call (*Nedayeh Aghaz*)

Where are my shoes?
Who was calling 'Sohrab'?
The voice was friendly, like air passing over a leaf.
My mother is asleep
So are Manouchehr, and Parvaneh, and maybe everyone else in town.
A June night flows over the seconds as quietly as a lament,
While a cool breeze steals my sleep from the green edge of the blanket.
The smell of departure is in the air.
My pillow is full of the song of swallows' feathers.

Morning will break
And to this bowl of water
The sky will emigrate.

I must leave tonight.

I, who from the most open of windows to the people of this quarter spoke,
But heard nothing about the quality of Time.
No eyes were fixed on the earth with passion.
No-one enchanted at the sight of a garden.
No-one took a magpie in some farm, seriously.
A gloom the size of a cloud seizes me
When from the window I see Houri,
The neighbour's young daughter
Reading jurisprudence
Under the rarest elm tree on earth.

But there are things and instances full of splendour,
(For example, I saw a poetess
So beguiled by the sight of space that the sky
Laid eggs in her eyes.)
On one of those nights
A man asked me:
'How many hours' walk until the ripening of grapes?'

Tonight I must go.
Tonight I must take a suitcase
The size of my shirt of solitude
And travel in a direction
Where epic trees can be seen,
Towards that wordless space that continually calls me.
Someone again called, 'Sohrab'!
My shoes, where are my shoes?

To the Garden of My Fellow Travellers (*Be Bagheh Ham Safaran*)

Call me.
You have a lovely voice.
Your voice is the green heart of that amazing plant
Growing at the limits of the intimacy of sorrow.

In the expanse of this dark age
I am more lonely than the taste of a song in the
uncomprehending street.
Come, let me tell you of the enormity of my loneliness
Which did not foresee the magnitude
of your sudden, unexpected attack.
But this is the nature of *ishq*.

There is no one here,
Come, let us steal life, then,
Between two encounters, divide it.
Together, let us understand something of the condition of stones.
Let us see things more quickly.
Look, the fountain jets on the face of the pool clock
Change time and make it round.
Come, turn into water, like a word on the line of my silence.
Come, and on my palm melt the luminous, celestial body of *ishq*.

Keep me warm.
(Once, in the wilderness of Kashan, the clouds thickened
And it rained heavily.
I was very cold, but behind a stone
The stove of the poppies kept me warm.)

In these dark streets
I fear the outcome of conflict between a striking match and hesitation.
I fear the cement-surfaced century.
Come, for me not to fear cities where black earth
serves as pasture of tall cranes.
Like a door, open me to the fall of a pear, in this age
of ascending steel.
Under a branch put me to sleep,
far from the night of clashing metals.
If the discoverer of the mine of morning arrives, call me,
And I, in the blooming of a jasmine through your fingers,
shall awaken.
Then
Tell me of bombs that fell while I slept.
Of cheeks drenched in tears while I slept.
Say how many ducks flew off the water.
In that turmoil where tanks trampled over children's dreams.

At the foot of which feeling of tranquillity did
the canary tie the yellow string of its song?
Say how many virgins arrived at the harbour.
What knowledge of music did the smell of gunpowder gain?
What understanding of the unknown taste
of bread appeared on the palate of prophesy?
Then I, like a faith warmed by the radiance of the equator,
At the initiation of a garden shall seat you.

Friend (*Doust*)

> *I should be glad of another death* (TS Eliot)

She was remarkable,
A child of her times,
In touch with far-reaching horizons,
Attuned to the music of water, of earth.

Her voice,
Like the anxious sadness of reality.
Her eyelashes
Showed us
The flow of elemental heartbeats.
Her hands
Leafed through
The clear air of generosity
And thrust kindness towards us.

She was in the guise of her own solitude.
The most passionate currents of her time
To the mirror she explained.
And like rain, was full of the freshness of reiteration,
And like trees,
In the wellbeing of light, unfolded.

Always summoned the childhood of wind,
Always entwined strands of speech
With a link to water.
For us, one night,
The green prostration of love
She so plainly displayed
That we stroked the feelings of the earth's surface
And like the expression of a pail of water, were refreshed.

Many a time we saw
With how many baskets
She went to pick a bough of blessings.

But it was not possible
For her simply to sit facing the clarity of the doves.
She went to the edge of nothingness
And lay down behind the forbearance of the lights
And thought not at all
That we, in the anxiety of the opening and closing of doors
For the eating of an apple,
Were left completely alone.

Till the Wet Pulse of Morning (*Ta Nabzeh Kheeseh Sobh*)

What splendour in the generous giving of superficial things!
O noble cancer of seclusion!
May my superficiality be lavished on you!

Someone came and
Stretched my hand
Up to the sinews of heaven.
Someone came with the bright light of faith
At the centre of his shirt buttons.
With the dry grass of old verse
He wove windows.
Like the day before yesterday's thoughts, he was young.
His vocal chords
Full of the blue qualities of the seashore.
Someone came and took away my books.
Over my head he drew a ceiling of floral proportions.
He extended my afternoon with endless corridors.
Placed my table under the sacredness of rain.
Then, we sat.
We spoke of verdant moments.
Of words whose lives were spent in water.
Our opportunities under appropriate clouds, which
Like the giddy body of an untimely dove,
Had the shape of happiness.

It was midnight, the tumult of the fruits
Made the trees look strange.
The dewy drift of our dream was wasted.
Then,
Hands, at the start of the body, bathed.
Then, in the drenched depths of the garden elm
Morning broke.

FROM BOOK VIII

We are Nothing But a Gaze

(*Ma Heech, Ma Negah*)

Oh Fervour, Oh Ancient One (*Eye Shoor, Eye Quadeem*)

In the morning
The spirited spread of a feast
Cast a shady canopy on happiness.
My picture fell across the expanse of a calendar:
In the bend of childish obliqueness,
On the inclining leisure of a feast
I cried:
'What lovely weather!'
In my lungs was the clarity of the wings of all the
birds of the world.
How fresh water was
That day!
The wind, in sheer doggedness, had disappeared.
I had spread all my geometry homework
On the floor.
That day
A few triangles
Drowned in the water.
I
Was dazed.
I leapt over the mountain in the atlas:
'Hey, helicopters, to the rescue!'
Pity:
Mouthed words collapsed in the passage of the wind.

Oh fluttering of fervour, Oh strongest of forms!
The shadow of a drinking glass
To the thirst of this shattered friendship
Guide.

The Tender Time of Sand (*Waqteh Latifeh Chenne*)

Rain
Washed the borders of tranquillity.
I, with damp sand intended to play
Dreaming of colourful journeys.
I had mingled with the freedom of the sands.
I was homesick.

In the garden a familiar table was laid.
At the centre, something looked like luminous perception:
A bunch of grapes had veiled every taint.
The restoration of silence dazed me.
I could see that there are trees.
When there are trees it is evident that one must be.
One must be, for the incantation of the story to be followed through till the white text.
But,
What colourful disappointment!

Beyond the Waters (*Az Abha Be Ba'd*)

In the days
when Knowledge lived at the water's edge.
Man,
In the agreeable idleness of a pasture
was happy with deep blue philosophies.
He thought like the birds.
His pulse beat with the pulse of the trees.
He had succumbed to conditions set by poppies.
The broad concepts of the shore
collided in the depth of his words.
Man
Slept in the embrace of the elements.
At the approach of fear he awoke.

But sometimes
The strange song of maturity rang out
In the brittle joints of enjoyment
The knees of ascension would become water.
At that time
The finger of evolution remained alone
In the precise design of grief.

Both Line and Space (*Ham Satr, Ham Sepeed*)

It is morning.
The bird of purity sings.
Autumn, on the dense wall, is scattered.
The exhilarating behaviour of the sun
Makes the mass of corruption spring from sleep.
An apple in the latticed opportunity of the basket, rots.
A feeling, like the alienation of things,
passes over eyelids.
Between a tree and the green instant
The recurrence of deep blue blends with the longing for speech.

But,
Inviolable whiteness of paper!
The pulse of our letters,
Beats in the absence of the calligrapher's ink.
In ecstasy's memory, the attraction of forms is lost.

The book must be closed.
One must rise
And walk along the stretch of time,
Look at the flowers, hear the enigma.
One must run until the end of being.
Follow the scent of the soil of annihilation.
Arrive at the encounter of tree and God.
One must sit close to the unfolding,
Some place between rapture and illumination.

Ancient Text of Night (*Matneh Ghadeemeh Shab*)

You, between the green stars of speech!
The fig leaf of darkness
Tells of the purity of stone.
Longing for the image of a garden, the heart of water
Pines.
A daily apple
Tastes of an illusion in our mouth.
O ancient fear! Addressing you my fingers lose consciousness.
Tonight
My hands have no bounds:
Tonight from the mythical branches,
They pick fruits.
Tonight
Every tree has as many leaves as I have fears.
In the warmth of the meeting came the courage to speak.
O colourful beginnings!
My eyes, in the magic breeze keep safe.
I am still
Dreaming of the unknown endowments of the night.
I am still
Thirsting for latticed waters.
The buttons on my clothes
Are the colour of those prayers of magical ages.
In the pastures that preceded speech
Our final bodily feast was afoot.
I, at that feast, heard the music of the stars
In earthenware crockery.
My eyes were filled with the migration of magicians.
O oldest of old images of narcissi in the mirror of grief
Your enchantment captured and carried me away –
Till the sphere of completion?
Maybe.

In the fervour of speech let us drink the water of discernment.

In the diffused legacy of night
Runs the pure modesty of narration:
In ages before the rise of alphabets
Was a great gathering of all living things.
Among all the contestants
My jaw cracked with the pride of speech.
Then
I, who was knee deep
In the purity of the silence of things green
Washed hands and face in the contemplation of forms.
Then, in another season
My shoes, from the word 'dew'
Became wet.
Then, when I sat on a stone,
I could hear their migration from the soles of my feet.
Then I saw that the being of each branch
Avoided parts of my hands.

O unscripted night!
My handkerchief was full of raw, unplanned schemes.
Behind the walls of a heavy sleep
A bird, coming from the fellowship of darkness
Carried away my handkerchief.
The first sands of inspiration grated under my feet.
My blood became the welcoming, tender host of space.
My pulse swam among the elements.

O night...
No, what am I saying?
The cold body of the speaker
Melted in the warm radiance of the window.
My finger pointed at an endearing scene.

No Dolls in Our Days (*Bee Roozha Aroosak*)

This being that sits in the light of awareness
Like a tender, elegant sleep
Casts fresh, crisp words
On the eyelids of contemplation.
Its eyes
A denial of the green calendar of life.
Its face, like a slice of holiday time, is white.

For years this worshipping vitality,
Like established good luck,
Sat on Friday's knees.
In the mornings, my mother
Took a basket full of water for the yellow flowers
I, for the mouth of contemplation
Took the unripe fruit of inspiration

This 'body' that knew neither night nor day.
Behind the sloping garden of numbers
Like a legend, slept.
My thoughts, from a parting in isolation, touched it.
Behind its eyes my mind melted.
On its supreme forehead
Time was running out.
Behind the box trees the pages of Fridays
Were being torn to the right size.
This auction of friendship.
Like a branch of a coconut tree.
Showered some shade between me and
the bitterness of Saturdays.
Or, like a gentle attack,

Overran the citadel of my fears.
Its hand, like an extension of free time.
Next to my 'home work', disappeared.

(Where was reality more fresh?
I, who, infatuated by a painless form,
Sometimes, in the poverty stricken tray that was home
Had seen the luminous fruits of inspiration.
With the coming of speech the discourse grew louder
In the rotting of mud and meat
The pulse of my feelings raced.
The anxiety of the petunias
Engulfed my conscience with ecstasy.
The innovative dew of life
On stubble
Was shining.)

Someone must say something to this patient presence
Within the gradual movements of the garden.
Someone must comprehend this small-sized form,
Interpret his hand for the surrounding palpitations,
Sprinkle a drop of Time
On this un-addressed face.
Someone must take this simple, downright point
Around the sentiments of the elements.
Someone must come from behind the illuminated doors.

Listen! Someone runs over the eyelids of happenings:
A child comes to this side.

Eyes of a Rite of Passage (*Cheshmaneh Yek Obour*)

    The speckled butterflies of contemplation filled the sky.
    The reflection of a bird fell upon waters of fellowship.
    The season flew off the wall, along the expanse of instinct.
    The wind was blowing from the region of the green basket of generosity.

    The vine was enamoured with the grapes
    A child came to pick them,
    His pockets full of craving.
    (Oh spring of daring!
    Your reach has been erased in the shade
    of the pine trees of reflection.)
    From behind words the child ran
    To the soft grasses of desire,
    Went to the ever-present fishes.
    By the edge of the pool
    The lonely fish scales of life filled the child's blood.
    Then a thorn scratched his foot,
    The burning of the body ended on the grass.
    (Sources of security!
    The anxiety of the body subsides sweetly in you.)
    In the courtyard, the chirpings of the birds of day before yesterday
    Poured upon the forehead of his thoughts.
    A river, flowing from the foot of the box trees until creativity
    Carried the ignorant desires of the body with it.
    The child was going further away from his luscious portion.
    Under the baptismal rain of the season
    The dignity of growth
    From the branches of the peach tree fell upon his shirt.
    In the course of the pink-hued grief of things,
    The sands of serenity
    Glittered still.
    Behind the gradual fading of talents
    The patterns of the whirligigs disappeared.

The child asked the innermost heart of sadness:
'How far is it to the doll's sunset?'

A leaf, migrating from a branch, startled him.
His face sought refuge
Behind other flowers.

(One morning, in those days of contemplation,
I heard the migration of the toys
Under the southern boxwoods.
Then, in the heat
My hand was filled with a squashed bunch of grapes.
Then the ailment of water in ancient pools
Drew my thoughts to the point of weariness.
Later, in the burning fever of typhoid,
My hand reached the hidden dimensions of flowers.
The pleasant dust of feigned oblivion
Over palpable pebbles, was extinguished.
I
Came face to face with the ascension of trees.
With the spread of a raven's feathers in spring,
With the descent of a frog in the obscure virtues of water,
With the giddy sincerity of the fountain in the pond,
With the wet rising of a bucket from the unknown depths of a well.)

The child entered the cacophony of numbers.
(On Heaven, free of distress, prior to symmetry and conformity!
Drenched in longing, I run after the ways of those days.)
The child ascended the steps of sin.
A tremor ran over the surface of tranquillity.
The significance of the smile of discernment shrank.

Solitude of a Scene (*Tanhayeh Manzareh*)

Pine trees, much too tall.
Ravens, much too black.
The sky, somewhat blue.
Stone walls, contemplation, detachment.
Orchard paths extending to nothingess.
Rooftop gutters decked with birds.
Candid sun.
Contented soil.

As far as the eye could see,
The awareness of autumn was present.
How wonderful!

With a look full of dewy expression,
Like a sleep full of the green stammering of a garden,
Eyes reflecting chequered modesty.
Undecided eyelids
Like the anxious fingers of a traveller's sleep!
Under the wakefulness of river-bank willows
Companionship,
Like a handful of ashes, furtively,
Was strewn over the warmth of awareness.
Thought
Was slow.
Desire, far away
Like a bird that sang on the tree of stories.

Where in coming autumns,
Will an eloquent mouth
Talk about
Enjoyable journeys?

Towards the Beloved's Imaginings (*Samteh Khialeh Doust*)

The moon
Was the colour of the description of copper.
It rose, like the pain of understanding.
The cypress tree
Was the striking cry of soil.
The pine tree nearby,
Like the ultimate in understanding,
Threw its shade on the plain page of the season.
The dry Kufi script of the nests could be read.
From dark lands
Came the scent of perception, taking shape.
The Friend
Touched
The awareness, that like a net, covered everything,
Heard the flowing phrases of the river,
As if telling himself:
No speech is as clear as this.
I, by the bubbling spring
Thought:
Tonight
The path of the ascension of things is so smooth!

Here Always 'Teeh' (*Eenja Hameesheh Teeh*)

Midday.
The beginning of God.
The immaculate stretch of sand
Listened,
Heard the water's mythical utterances.
Water, like a look at the dimensions of perception,
A crane,
Like a happening in white,
Was at the edge of the pond,
Washing its alluring form
In the gaze of detachment.
The eye
Was arriving at the opportunity of water.
The taste of clean signals,
On the palate of the salt marsh, was being lost to memory.

How far over the Kavir
Is the green garden of nearness,
The pure face of a sweet sleep?

You,
Like a beautiful brief stay
In the sanctuary of the meadow of closeness!
In which direction of contemplation
Will colourful no-thingness
Cast a shadow?
When
Will humanity,
Like the song of bountiful generosity
In the speech of space be discovered?
Oh exquisite start!
Enchanted expressions still sorely missed!

Till the End in Audience (*Ta Enteha Hozour*)

Tonight,
In a strange dream
The door towards words
Will be opened.
The wind will have something to say.
An apple will fall,
Will roll on the earth,
And enter the absent land of Night.
The ceiling of a delusion will collapse.
The eye
Will see the sad consciousness of plants.
An ivy will wind around the contemplation of God.
The secret will overflow.
The roots of the piety of the age shall rot.
At the start of the road of darkness
The verge of the speech of water
Will glisten,
The innermost centre of the mirror will understand.

Tonight,
The stem of significance
Shall be shaken by the breath of the Friend.
Bewilderment shall fly away.

At night's end, an insect
Shall experience
Its fresh, green share of solitude.

Inside the word 'morning'
Morning will break.

Glossary

ASHEQ: One who is overcome by *ishq*.

HEECH: No-thing

HOURI: A girl with beautiful eyes, in this world but especially in Paradise

IRFAN: Mystical knowledge

ISHQ: Passionate mystical love for the Beloved, which for the mystic constitutes the driving force of life and evolution towards Truth and Reality

NOWRUZ: Iranian New Year (21st March)

SAMBOUSEK: Triangular parcels of dough, stuffed and cooked, served as starters

TANANA HA YA HOO: Meaningless words

TARS: Musical instruments